Editor's letter

"If you've just bought – or you're about to buy – a new TV, you'll be glad you opened this book. Although the letters "HD" are everywhere these days, you won't find many people willing to explain what HD really is. Even worse, if you're not careful, you can end up falling foul of the marketing and not getting the best out of what's a very real and welcome change to the way we enjoy TV, films and music in our homes.

Thankfully, here at iGIZMO we've done the hard work for you. From choosing and buying your ideal HD partner to setting it up in its new home (and making it look its very best), we'll cut through the marketing hype and arm you with the questions you need to ask both before *and* after you buy.

Kit yourself out with the right high-definition devices and you'll reap incredible rewards. After thousands of hours of testing, we'll delve into all the options, from next-generation DVDs, to the best surround-sound setups and networked home devices."

Welcome to the HD revolution!

Editor

Sign up for the free magazine at www.igizmo.co.uk/signup...

... and see more online at www.igizmo.co.uk

BOOKAZINES

HDTV
and home entertainment

Turned on to
technology

iGIZMO

Contents

HDTV
and home entertainment

HD is the buzzword of the moment, but the marketing all too often glosses over what "high definition" really means – sometimes deliberately. If you're unsure of the difference between HD capable and HD ready, or between standard and high definition for that matter, you're in the right place. We'll also be seeing why now's such a good time to get a new TV as the UK switches over to digital broadcasts – happening sooner than you'd think.

Why HD?

There's a revolution coming – and it will be televised. But what's everyone getting so excited about?

Old Skool: CRT-based TVs are big, power-hungry and low-resolution

The good news is that if you're reading this, there's a good chance you've already got some idea of what HDTV is. And even if you haven't, the basics are actually pretty simple. At its most fundamental, it simply means that the number of elements (pixels) used in your TV picture is increased, leading to better-looking pictures and lots more detail.

Why? Well, if anything, we should be asking why it hasn't happened before, as the technical quality of TV broadcasts hasn't gone up significantly in decades. DVDs and the switch to digital broadcasting (*see p16*) have improved matters, but the sad truth is that old-fashioned "standard definition" just doesn't cut it on today's bigger sets.

What's now thought of as an "old-fashioned" TV uses a cathode-ray tube, an invention which has served us well since TV's introduction in the early 20th century. But it's rapidly becoming a fuzzy dinosaur when compared to flat-panel LCD or plasma TVs. Because of the way it works, cathode-ray technology results in a cabinet that extends

nearly as far back as it does across. Not only does that restrict where you can actually put it, but also the physical upper limit of how big a TV screen can be.

Flat panels, on the other hand, measure just a few inches or less thick, and yet can reach screen sizes well in excess of 100in. They're capable of being much higher definition, with each pixel being individually controllable. By comparison, the picture on a CRT is made up of horizontal lines, created by firing an electron gun at a screen covered in sulphur – an imprecise process invented well over a hundred years ago.

Size is everything

So the switch from CRT means you can fit a much larger screen in your lounge than you could before, with 32in panels fitting comfortably into the average room, and 60in monsters within the reach of enthusiasts. Combine that with the increase in detail, though, and you've got problems. Watch a TV broadcast (or even a DVD) on these larger

> "Besides seeing bags more detail, expect more realistic colours and better handling of movement"

Even if you've bought an HD-ready TV you're happy with, you're not necessarily out of the woods yet...

screens, and you'll soon realise what broadcasters have been getting away with on fuzzy CRTs for years. The low resolution and dull images aren't a pretty sight.

So that's where high definition content comes in. Besides seeing bags more lovely detail, the increased amount of information used means you can also expect more realistic colours, better handling of movement and crisper edges. And that's not all – there are other changes happening in both UK broadcasting and the world of electronics that make this a good time to ditch that big old box in the corner.

First, the UK (along with much of the rest of the world) is switching over to digital TV broadcasts sooner rather than later, and you'll need to get a digital tuner (if you don't

already have one) before the analogue signal is switched off for good. And while most of the free TV channels we're used to won't actually be switching to high definition for a while yet, it's beginning to happen, and getting the right set now means you'll be ready for them when they do.

But before you rush out and buy any old box – either because it's the most expensive or the cheapest – allow us a few more pages of your time: TV manufacturers know they're on to a good thing and, with the market so competitive, a trip to a TV showroom can be a baffling experience. Higher numbers aren't always better and there are plenty of pitfalls.

Even if you've bought an HD-ready TV you're happy with, you're not necessarily out of the woods yet. Getting the HD content you want isn't as easy as it could be, and there are some big (not to mention expensive) decisions you'll need to make before you'll get the best that modern home entertainment can offer – decisions we'll be dedicating the rest of this book to.

Modern times: With more pixels and bigger sizes, newer TVs show up detail

HD FAQ

We dispel some of the myths surrounding HD, and tackle people's most immediate questions and concerns

WHAT'S THE DIFFERENCE BETWEEN DIGITAL AND HD?

Digital TV is replacing traditional analogue broadcasts in the UK by 2012 – see more about it over the page. It's less prone to interference and can carry many more channels than the old analogue system. In future, broadcasts will be both HD and digital. HD simply refers to a picture's resolution.

AND WHAT'S THE DIFFERENCE BETWEEN HD CAPABLE, HD READY AND FULL HD?

This question is a good example of how something that's intended to make things simple does exactly the opposite. Those pesky stickers you'll see plastered on TVs and other equipment denote which standards of HD content a device can cope with – it doesn't necessarily mean it will show everything at the best possible quality. Take a look at p14 to find out exactly what you're getting.

HOW MANY DIFFERENT FORMATS ARE THERE, THEN?

Getting an HDTV is a bit like getting a coffee at Starbucks. Aside from the different sizes and flavours, some of the terminology used is baffling if you haven't seen it before. We'll be explaining what it all means, though, so it won't be long before you can order a 24f, 1080p Frappacinolatte with confidence.

WILL I NEED A NEW TV TO WATCH HD?

That depends – if you've got a huge cathode-ray set in the corner of your lounge, it's going to have to go. If you're lucky enough to have a flatscreen TV already, you should be set, although chances are it could do with setting up and attaching to some decent programming before it will look its best. And if you've got a reasonably modern PC, you're in for a treat (see p80).

WHY CAN'T I USE MY BIG OLD TV?

There's nothing to stop you hooking up Sky HD or a Blu-ray drive to your old cathode-ray TV, but unless it's an incredibly expensive example it probably won't display the images all that well; more likely, it'll look terrible. Flat-panel TVs (whichever technology they use) simply show more information than cathode-ray TVs, and it's only with one of these you'll get HD looking at its very best.

SHOULD I GO FOR A PLASMA OR LCD TV?

Good question. Both have their relative advantages and foibles – take a look at p22 to find out which is right for you. But the most important thing is getting the right size and resolution (see p20), and ensuring it has the features that you'll actually find useful.

WHAT'S THIS ABOUT A FORMAT WAR?

There was a pitched battle between Blu-ray and its rival format, HD DVD, which many think stifled the HD disc market. Either way, it's over now, with HD DVD production having ceased and Blu-ray the official winner.

HD COMES WITH EVIL COPY PROTECTION, DOESN'T IT?

Yes, but there's no need to be paranoid about it. Some HD broadcasts are encoded in a way to prevent them being recorded, and there are multiple technologies used on Blu-ray discs to stop them from being copied. The only thing to worry about is HDCP on older systems (*see p83*).

YOU CAN'T GET HD IN THE UK, CAN YOU?

It's true that there aren't many HD broadcasters in the UK yet – Freeview is still in standard definition, for example, and will remain so for a while yet. You'll need a satellite dish or cable supplier for now (Sky and Virgin Media both operate HD services), but there are plenty of other ways of getting HD content, some of which are free (*see p66*).

WILL I NEED A NEW AERIAL, TOO?

If you get HD over cable or satellite, then no, but if you want to watch Freeview at its best on your HD set you may need to upgrade your rooftop aerial, or at least boost the signal. Digital coverage is also patchy in some parts of the country – take a look at *www.digitaluk.co.uk* to find out about the signal quality where you live.

ISN'T DVD HD?

Sadly not. While it's much better than VHS, DVD has a lower resolution than even the lowest-quality HD video. Its recording capability is too low for full-length HD films, too – hence the introduction of higher capacity Blu-ray discs, which store between five and ten times more (*see p70*).

IF HD'S SO BRILLIANT, WHY ARE MERE STANDARD-DEFINITION PRODUCTS MENTIONED IN THESE PAGES?

As much as we wish everything was in HD, SD isn't going anywhere in a hurry. So to get the best out of your HDTV, you need to make sure that both the source and your TV are the very best possible for both standards.

Understanding HD formats

With a galaxy of woolly marketing terms such as "HD ready" and "HD capable", it's all too easy to become confused by HDTV

Like many new technologies, HDTV can become horribly confusing. Sadly, it isn't always helped by attempts to simplify it. Visit a couple of websites or pop into a shop and you'll see a myriad of meaningless marketing terms and logos, and you'll be lucky if you can find someone to explain what it all means.

Unfortunately, you can't trust the simple rule of bigger numbers being better, either: 720p, for example, is in some ways better than 1080i, and understanding why is crucial to making the right buying decision.

Making new resolutions
Unlike the standard TV we've enjoyed for all these years in the UK, HDTV actually comes in several versions of varying quality. The three main ones worthy of consideration are known as 720p, 1080i and 1080p. The "i" suffix stands for interlaced and the "p" for progressive.

The numeric part that comes before the letter refers to the number of horizontal lines that make up the picture. The broadcast standard that's been used in the UK for the last 40 years, known as PAL, has 576 lines, so adding an extra 144 lines (for 720p) or an extra 504 lines (for 1080p) means there's the potential to display significantly more detail, which is why HDTV programmes look so good.

Once you factor in horizontal pixels, the difference is even starker. The total number of pixels in a 720p image is 1280 x 720, which equals 921,600. 1080i and 1080p images generally have a resolution of 1920 x 1080, giving an astonishing 2,073,600 pixels. By contrast, a PAL TV image has just 720 pixels across and 576 pixels vertically, equating to a mere 414,720 elements. And in the US, where HDTV is a few years ahead of us, the old NTSC standard has even fewer lines: 720 across and just 480 vertically.

Progressive vs interlaced
Video signals are made up of a series of frames, which are flashed onto the screen sequentially to give the impression of movement. With interlaced video, the frame is split into two "fields", with all the odd lines (1, 3, 5, 7...) of an image shown first, and then the even lines an instant later to fill in the gaps and make up the full picture. In order to display 25 frames every second – which is required to give the effect of smooth motion – there need to be 50 fields for every second in the original video.

With progressively displayed video, on the other hand, all of the lines of each frame are displayed simultaneously. For a 720p video to be displayed at 25fps, there only needs to be 25 complete fields for each second of footage, rather than the 50 split fields that are required for an interlaced video.

Progressive scan video is capable of better quality than interlaced video, as the de-interlacing process can leave fast movement appearing jerky. And while a good-quality HDTV should generally be good enough at this process to leave you wondering what the fuss is about, some content will certainly suffer. So while interlaced video will be fine for more gentle wildlife documentaries, it isn't so well suited to sports where the players (or balls) are moving around quickly.

The reason interlaced video is historically so popular is because it requires much lower bandwidth. Progressive scan transmits much more data at once, so a larger "pipe" is needed to transmit it. Sadly, that leaves 720p and 1080i as the dominant forces in HDTV, with the US in particular coming heavily down on the side of the latter.

Upscaling
It's important to remember that, while your HDTV may be able to support 720p, 1080i and 1080p, you're still dependent on the source to match this quality, and there's little guarantee what will happen if it doesn't. Your Blu-ray player will most likely output 1080p video, while HD broadcasters such as Sky, Virgin and the BBC mainly use 1080i, but also 720p. Games consoles such as the Xbox 360 and PlayStation 3 can be set to output 720p or 1080p.

Your HDTV is likely to have a resolution of either 1366 x 768 or 1920 x 1080. Both will happily show 720p content, but video with 1080 lines has to be downscaled – or shrunk – to fit on a screen with physically fewer lines. This should be done fairly transparently, and a decent TV will resize the incoming video without you noticing any big drop in quality, but it's by no means guaranteed. Cheaper sets may simply go blank when presented with such a task.

Upscaling capability is also important, because you're likely to be watching a good deal of SD content on your TV for the foreseeable future and, again, you'll generally get what you pay for when it comes to quality. For more on that, take a look at p72. ©

FAQ

IS 1080P THE BEST HD VIDEO THERE IS?
No, 1080p might be called Full HD, but this is slightly misleading, as it isn't the highest resolution that exists for video. 2160p – also known as Quad HD – has a resolution of 3840 x 2160, four times the resolution of 1080p. Japan Broadcasting has also demonstrated 4320i, which has an interlaced resolution of 7860 x 4320. It's already being talked up as the next big thing, but don't expect to see video like this coming to an HDTV near you anytime soon.

	Resolution	HDTV	Standard/widescreen	Progressive scan
Standard UK TV	Up to 576 visible lines	✗	Both	✗
DVD	720 x 576	✗	Both	✓
720p	1280 x 720	✓	✗/✓	✓
1080i	1920 x 1080	✓	✗/✓	✗
1080p	1920 x 1080	✓	✗/✓	✓

"Unfortunately, you can't trust the simple rule of bigger numbers being better..."

BRAVIA

480i/p DV NTSC

PAL 576i/p

720p

1080i/p

Consumer HDV 1440x1080

SONY

The terms you need to know...

You might see one or more of the following terms used to describe a TV's HD credentials, along with their commensurate shiny stickers on the front. Some of these are more "official" than others, and you might see the odd variation on them, too – so make sure you find out the specifics beforehand.

■ **HD COMPATIBLE:** This term is used to indicate that an HDTV has an HDMI input, but if this is as far as it goes, it will almost certainly have fewer than 720 lines. As such, it isn't ideal for playing back HD content (it will just end up downscaled), but if you're looking for a second, smaller set (sub-24in), it may still be a perfectly good choice.

■ **HD READY:** EICTA, the European Information and Communications Technology Industry Association, requires that panels sporting an HD ready logo must be able to display a 1280 x 720 pixel image at 50/60Hz progressive scan (720p). It should also include a component video input, plus either HDMI or DVI, which needs to support HDCP (High Definition Content Protection). Some (but not all) HD-ready TVs will still handle a 1080p video source by downscaling the signal to 720p.

■ **FULL HD:** A label that's employed to indicate a resolution of at least 1920 x 1080 pixels – theoretically as good as it gets. Anything with this label should therefore be capable of displaying 1080i and 1080p video at full quality, without any downscaling. And while that's better in theory, remember that there's more to image quality than sheer number of pixels. You'll also generally pay more for a Full HD set, which is why it's such a popular sticker with manufacturers...

The digital switchover

The UK is about to switch over to digital broadcasting, making now the perfect time to cast off your analogue roots and embrace the future of TV viewing

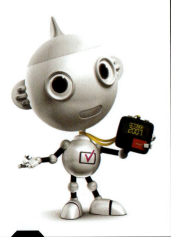

Over the next five years, the analogue television signals that have served the UK's homes since the BBC's first test broadcasts in 1929 will be switched off. By the end of 2012, the UK (with the exception of the Channel Islands) will be completely digital.

More than eight out of ten households in the UK are already watching digital television, be it through Sky satellite, Virgin Media's cable network, a Freeview box, Freesat or one of the new television services being delivered over the internet, such as BT Vision. However, that still leaves a sizeable chunk of the country potentially facing blank screens. So why is the government so keen to switch off the old analogue signal?

Around one in four households in the UK are currently unable to receive Freeview digital channels through their television aerial, because the digital signal has to be choked back to prevent it from interfering with the analogue picture. By switching off the analogue channels, the digital signal can be boosted, giving almost 99% of the population access to the dozens of television and radio channels afforded by digital broadcasting.

The analogue signal switch-off has already begun, with viewers in the Border region being the first to complete the switchover. So before it's too late, now's a good time to start checking your TV equipment is ready.

While the vast majority have access to digital television on their main, living-room television, there are another 35 million secondary sets in bedrooms and kitchens across the country – and only 10 million of those have been converted to digital, according to the latest figures from Ofcom.

Several solutions

The good news is you don't have to throw out your old sets. All but the most ancient of televisions can be connected to a Freeview set-top box, which costs as little as £10 nowadays, or from £40 for a Freesat setup. As far as subscription services go, both Sky and Virgin Media also offer "multiroom" packages, where you can get extra satellite or cable boxes for the bedroom.

Practically every new HDTV will have one or more digital TV tuners built into them, but to ensure customers don't accidentally pick up an old-fashioned analogue-only set shortly before switch off, high-street stores such as Currys and Comet have pledged to stop selling them a year before your region goes digital.

Don't be fooled into paying more than you have to: many people confuse digital with HD, but you don't actually need an HD set to receive digital, and there are no HD channels even available on Freeview as it stands. To review your HD TV broadcast options, switch over to p66. ⓖ

↻ WHEN WILL I BE SWITCHED OFF?

Region	Date
Border	2008-2009
West Country, Granada	2009
Wales	2009-2010
West, STV North, STV Central	2010-2011
Central, Yorkshire, Anglia	2011
Meridian, London, Tyne Tees, Ulster	2011-12

GRAMPIAN

SCOTTISH

TYNE TEES

BORDER

ULSTER

GRANADA

YORKSHIRE

HTV WALES

CENTRAL

ANGLIA

CARLTON/LWT

HTV WEST

MERIDIAN

WEST COUNTRY

CHANNEL

Stop! Before you rush out and buy the biggest, most expensive set you can, take a look at the next few pages. Not only could it save you a packet, but there's also an art to getting the right size and type of TV – it's not always obvious what you're getting when looking in the shop or online. Should you go for LCD or plasma? Or how about an HD projector? We'll take you through the options, how the technology works, and what type of TV should fill that yawning HD gap in your life.

19

Which size and resolution?

Getting the size and resolution of your TV right is essential, and with choices ranging from 7in to 150in, there are a baffling number of choices

The chart with axes:
- Y-axis: Maximum optimum viewing distance (in feet), 0 to 20
- X-axis: Screen size (in inches), 23, 27, 32, 37, 42, 46, 50, 60, 70

Legend:
- STANDARD DEFINITION (red)
- 720P HD (dark blue)
- 1080P (yellow)

Before you start traipsing around the shops or flicking through brochures, take the time to make a few key decisions. That way, when you start looking for your HD screen, you'll be fully prepared and able to navigate through the bewildering maze of model numbers and fancy-sounding features. We'll cover all of those decisions in this chapter, and the first comes down to size; namely, how big a TV your room (or spouse) can take. Thankfully, one of these is a science.

First of all, there's the sheer physical space you've got to play with. HDTVs have a widescreen aspect ratio and, like traditional sets, are measured in inches diagonally. So a 32in screen would measure approximately 28in (71cm) wide and 16in (40cm) high. A plasma screen will then be anything up to 8in deep, with LCDs tending to be much slimmer.

But while that means most homes will accommodate a much bigger flat-panel screen than they would a boxy old CRT, don't just go for the biggest set you can afford or can fit in without removing a window: besides looking silly, too big a set in too small a room will be wasted, as you'll simply be sitting too close to appreciate it.

Supersize me

You should also set yourself some lower limits. Despite what some would have you believe, you do need a relatively large screen to appreciate the full effect of full-blown HDTV. Yes, HD content will look great on a 23in screen, but you'll often be hard-pushed to tell it from a decent standard-definition picture – a wasted opportunity in our book.

To really appreciate even the lowliest 720p standard, a 32in diagonal is about the minimum, and for full 1080p you're looking at more like 48in before the difference is truly noticeable. Despite that, you'll see LCDs as small as 37in boasting 1080p resolutions. That's all well and good, but remember you'll be paying extra for it.

The final resolution

Apart from size, the other factor to consider is the TV's native resolution – essentially, the number of pixels it can display. Plasma and, to a lesser extent, LCD screens come in a variety of actual resolutions, but the very least an HDTV

needs to be is 720 vertical pixels (HD ready) or 1080 vertical pixels high to be Full HD. While LCDs will generally then have at least 1280 horizontal pixels across the screen, it's fairly common for plasmas to have fewer: 1024 pixels isn't unusual for an HD-ready plasma, for example.

But also bear in mind that while a higher-resolution TV might be more tempting, it's not the be all and end all. Not only is that extra resolution wasted below a certain size, but the ability to handle motion smoothly and reproduce a wide, natural range of colours is just as important. So if budget is tight, go for a decent 720p set rather than a lower-end 1080p one. Its ability to handle picture detail is likely to be much better, as is your overall viewing experience.

Room with a view

It's just as important to consider the room you're actually buying the set for. Consider how far away you'll be sitting from it, the furniture or wall you might put it on, and pay special attention to elements such as radiators and potentially distracting window reflections.

Sit close up to a 720p 28in TV, and far away from a 1080p 50in set and you may not be able to notice the difference in quality between the two. Likewise, buy a large screen with a low resolution and sit too close, and you'll simply end up seeing all the individual pixels that HD is all about hiding.

The chart

The chart above shows the viewing distance at which it's generally possible to see the benefits of 720p and 1080p compared to standard definition for a range of screen sizes. In order to decide what size TV you should get, first work out how far away you'll be sitting from your set, then weigh up whether you want to splash out the extra on a 1080p-capable one.

For example, if your sofa will be about six and a half feet from your TV, a standard-definition TV above 23in will start to expose individual pixels (assuming you have 20/20 vision). By contrast, on a TV with 720p resolution, the screen would have to be larger than 32in to make out the pixels, and with a 1080p set you could stretch to a 50in model before you start seeing anything like individual dots. ©

Higher resolutions mean you can sit closer to your TV without seeing the individual elements that make up the picture.

Which technology to choose?

Having trouble picking whether you want an LCD TV or a plasma screen? Our expert guide will take you through the pros and cons

LCD TV

☑ LCD PROS

CONSUMER CHOICE LCDs are the more popular technology, designed with consumers in mind. As such, they come with built-in TV tuners, a good balance of inputs, and a wider range of sizes and models, from 7in all the way up to 100in-plus giants. New sets are arriving every year.

POWER-SAVING LCDs use less power than a plasma set of the same size, so will be cheaper to run. They also run cooler, so you don't need noisy cooling fans.

SLIMMER & LIGHTER As LCD panels are lighter and slimmer than plasmas, they're easier to handle and offer a far greater range of stand and wall-mounting options.

CHEAPER LCD is currently the more affordable technology up to sizes of 37in and, if you want smaller, there's no other choice. The price gap with plasmas is growing, too.

LESS REFLECTIVE While LCDs generally have lower brightness and contrast than plasmas, the lack of a glass front means they're less prone to distracting reflections, making them the better choice under normal lighting conditions.

RELIABILITY Modern LCD TVs should comfortably outlast a CRT. Over long periods of time, the backlight will slightly fade, but the rate of decline is slow and the backlight should last longer than the product's usable lifetime.

☒ LCD CONS

LIMITED SIZE If you want a very big screen (greater than 42in), LCD TVs get prohibitively expensive and you won't currently find any as large as the very biggest plasmas.

RESPONSE TIMES LCD wasn't originally developed to show moving images, and motion handling is still one of its weakest points. It's been all but solved on most sets, but cheaper units may still show ghosting or motion blur on fast-moving action. Check before you buy.

LESS ROBUST As LCDs don't have any glass to protect the screen, knocking them can cause real damage – a potential problem if the kids want to give Barney the dinosaur a hug, or decide to join in with some drawing...

NOT SO BLACK These days, the biggest complaint about LCD is its difficulty in producing truly dark blacks, leading to lower overall contrast than plasma. Since there's always a backlight switched on, the best many LCDs can do (without reducing overall picture quality) is a very dark grey. When you're watching dark, atmospheric films, this doesn't make the most of subtlety. Less of problem that it was, though.

TOO MUCH CHOICE As the technology du jour, every company and its dog is producing panels – of vastly varying quality and price. And while that means competition is fierce, the number of options can be bewildering.

PLASMA TV

☑ PLASMA PROS

LARGER SCREENS The primary advantage of plasma TVs is that they come in much bigger screen sizes than LCD, and at some very attractive prices. If you want a 42in screen or larger, you'll find that plasmas currently offer by far the better value for money.

HIGH CONTRAST While absolute picture quality is similar to LCD, plasmas generally exhibit superior brightness and contrast. If you can avoid lights reflecting off the glass screen and into your field of vision, you'll be rewarded with richer colours, darker blacks and cleaner whites.

MOTION HANDLING Like CRTs before them, plasmas are great at displaying motion, so you'll get smoother action on your screen than with LCD. For gaming or movies, this can make a big difference.

LONG LIFE Contrary to popular opinion, modern plasmas are just as reliable as LCDs and CRTS, and should last for around 60,000 hours of use. Once they break, they're difficult to service (like CRTs), so you're likely to need a new set. For average viewing, though, they should last for well over a decade.

☒ PLASMA CONS

INDUSTRY PANELS Not all plasmas are designed for home use, so check the specs carefully. Some of the keenest prices are on models designed for public display, which have just a PC input and no TV tuner. If you want to connect your normal peripherals, you may also need to buy an input box, which can be costly.

RESOLUTION The HD ready specification only states the number of lines a display has to have (a minimum vertical resolution of 720), but nothing about the horizontal resolution. The resolution of 720p footage is 1280 pixels wide by 720 pixels high, but some plasma screens have non-standard resolutions such as 1024 x 768. To achieve the widescreen aspect ratio, the horizontal pixels are non-square. As such, they won't display HD material pixel for pixel and, while the difference can be hard to spot, it can at times adversely affect the image.

BURN-IN Like CRTs, plasma screens are susceptible to burn-in, where a static image displayed for too long can leave a ghostly outline, permanently burnt into the phosphor coating. It's less of a problem with the latest screens (particularly if they're set up properly – see p56), but still something to be wary of.

BULKY PANELS The technology used in plasma screens makes them much heavier than LCDs, so wall-mounting can be a problem. You'll likely need stronger brackets and better support for stands, and you may feel happier consulting a professional.

POWER GUZZLERS As plasma is essentially supercharged gas, it's no surprise that the process kicks out a fair bit of heat. Many need fans to keep them cool, which is a potential source of distracting noise. Power usage varies depending on the brightness of the scene, too, and can be very high.

PROJECT X

LCD and plasma aren't the only ways to get HD into your life – and there's no denying the thrill of using a **projector** to bring the big screen into your home. With the ability to get massive pictures for competitive prices, it's certainly worth considering – we've rounded up the best of the crop on p116.

But while projectors are great for the cinema experience, they aren't ideal for watching TV. For starters, most home cinema projectors don't have the brightness to be watched in a normally lit room, and they're also comparatively expensive to run. You'll have to replace the bulb at some point, and this can cost £200 in itself.

You may also have come across **rear-projection TVs**. These combine a screen and projector in a TV-style box, and cost less for big screen sizes than either LCD or plasma. They're much better for watching TV than pure projectors and their bulbs last longer, too, although most struggle under bright lighting and colours simply aren't as rich as with LCD or plasmas. But they're also very bulky and, while they're popular in the US (where rooms are generally bigger), most UK homes simply don't have the space. LCD and plasma TVs are, therefore, a better choice.

SUMMARY

These days, there's little to separate LCD and plasma screens when it comes to image quality. If you can get to a shop, we'd recommend comparing the two for yourself with one of your own favourite DVDs. This will let you choose between the two technologies based on your viewing material rather than the flattering imagery the shop will be using.

For most people, though, the choice will come down to size and value. If you're getting a TV up to 37in in size, then LCD is better value, and there's plenty of choice. If you want a 42in or bigger screen, plasmas have the cost advantage and should be your first port of call. But don't get too hung up on one technology or the other – finding the correct size and feature set is ultimately more important when finding the HD partner of your dreams.

How it works: LCD

Liquid crystal displays have been around for decades, and the technology is now so advanced it can create stunning images

TFT glass A thin film of silicon is coated onto the glass to provide each pixel with a transistor switch – the Thin Film Transistor.

Diffuser This white panel scatters the light from the backlight and ensures it's distributed evenly.

Colour filter This controls the amount of red, green and blue light that's displayed by each pixel.

Backlight Most LCD screens use cold cathode fluorescent lamps above, beside and sometimes behind the LCD to provide a light source.

Liquid crystal

LCD TVs work by shining a light behind a screen made up of two thin, polarised panels that sandwich a liquid-crystal gel between them. That gel is divided into an X/Y grid of the required number of pixels. In the case of an LCD TV, each pixel is then divided horizontally into three subpixels – red, green and blue – which together produce a white pixel.

The liquid crystals that form the gel are affected by electric current. A common type of crystal used in LCD TVs, called Twisted Nematics (TN), is naturally twisted, whereas other types twist when an electric current is applied. By varying the voltage to each crystal, it can be made to twist or straighten to varying degrees, affecting the passage of light through it.

Doing the twist

By applying an electric current to each subpixel, it's possible to control both the brightness of the pixel and its colour. In order to control the individual pixels, each one has a transistor switch, known as a Thin Film Transistor, which is why you'll sometimes hear TVs (or computer monitors, which work in exactly the same way) called TFTs.

Different types of crystal exhibit different properties: some will allow better viewing angles, whereas others will deliver greater contrast (the amount of backlight they can block/let through with their range of movement). Various techniques are used to overcome the potential shortcomings of each, leading to a wide range of proprietary processing brand names (*see p34*).

There are a number of other factors affecting the quality of the resulting display. Not just its resolution (the number of pixels), but also the strength of the backlight, the quality of the electronics controlling the pixels, and the physical speed at which the pixels can move from one state to another. The latter is known as response time, and affects how well the panel displays movement. ⓘ

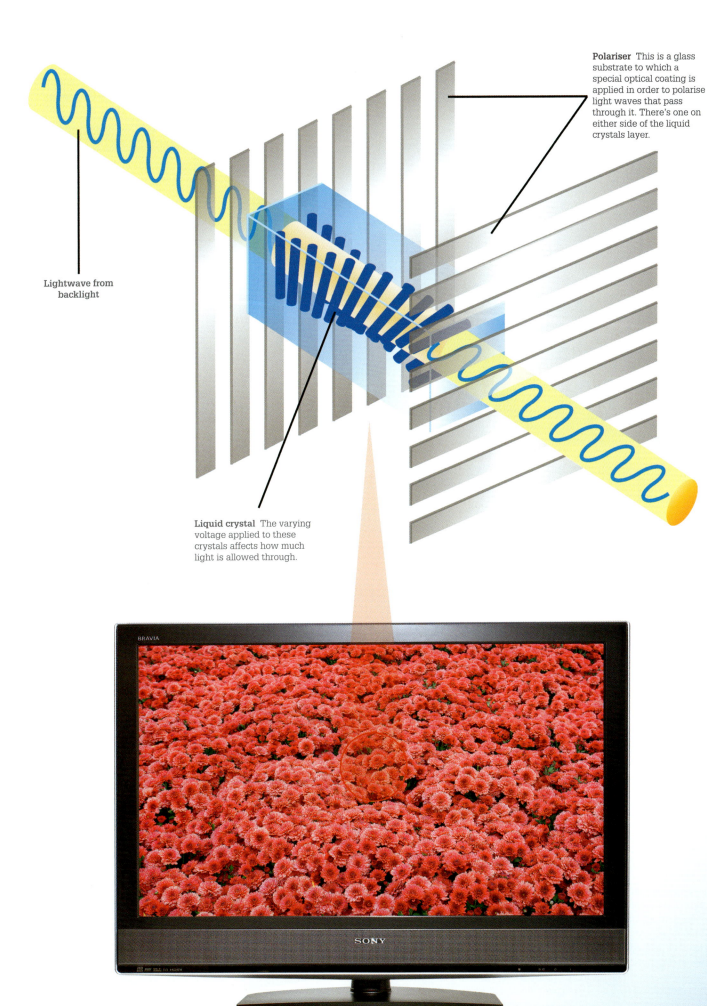

Polariser This is a glass substrate to which a special optical coating is applied in order to polarise light waves that pass through it. There's one on either side of the liquid crystals layer.

Lightwave from backlight

Liquid crystal The varying voltage applied to these crystals affects how much light is allowed through.

How it works: plasma

Plasma displays may look much the same as LCDs, but they work in a slightly different way, which has implications on their qualities and price

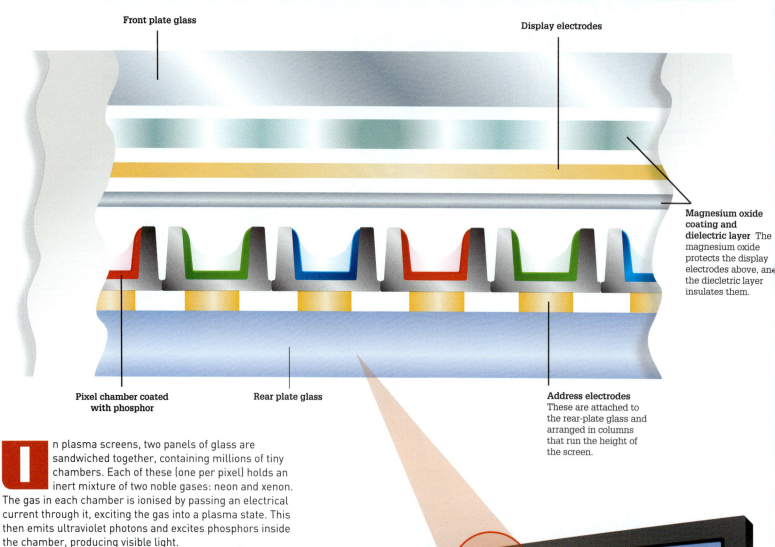

Front plate glass

Display electrodes

Magnesium oxide coating and dielectric layer The magnesium oxide protects the display electrodes above, and the diecletric layer insulates them.

Pixel chamber coated with phosphor

Rear plate glass

Address electrodes These are attached to the rear-plate glass and arranged in columns that run the height of the screen.

In plasma screens, two panels of glass are sandwiched together, containing millions of tiny chambers. Each of these (one per pixel) holds an inert mixture of two noble gases: neon and xenon. The gas in each chamber is ionised by passing an electrical current through it, exciting the gas into a plasma state. This then emits ultraviolet photons and excites phosphors inside the chamber, producing visible light.

To create colours, each pixel chamber is further split into three subpixels. Each of these is coated with a different colour phosphor: red, green and blue. By controlling the voltage applied to each subpixel, it's possible to control the level of red, green and blue light emitted, and thus the brightness and colour of each pixel's output.

All blacks

Unlike LCDs, there's no constant backlight to block out, so plasmas are able to display truer blacks. And as they're also capable of equally bright whites, they usually end up with a greater contrast than LCDs can manage. The gas naturally reacts more quickly to changes in voltage than liquid crystals, too, so the rendition of movement across a screen can be handled more smoothly.

The downside is that – like CRTs before them – plasmas are susceptible to burn-in, with the light-emitting phosphors losing their luminosity with use. So, when an image, such as a TV channel logo, is displayed in the same position for prolonged periods, it can end up permanently etched in the same place. It's less of an issue these days with modern sets, but you should carefully follow manufacturers' advice on how to avoid it. ⓖ

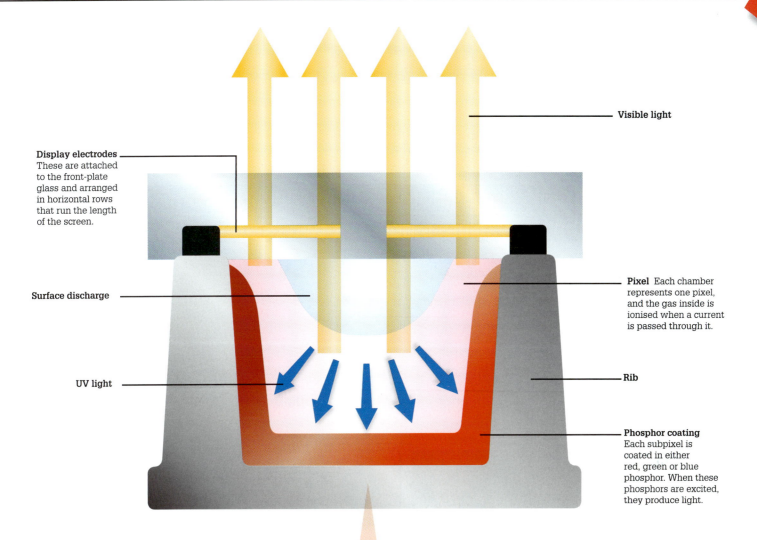

Visible light

Display electrodes These are attached to the front-plate glass and arranged in horizontal rows that run the length of the screen.

Surface discharge

UV light

Pixel Each chamber represents one pixel, and the gas inside is ionised when a current is passed through it.

Rib

Phosphor coating Each subpixel is coated in either red, green or blue phosphor. When these phosphors are excited, they produce light.

How it works: projectors

Projector manufacturers dazzle potential buyers with promised benefits of their chosen technology. Here's how the two main types work

DLP

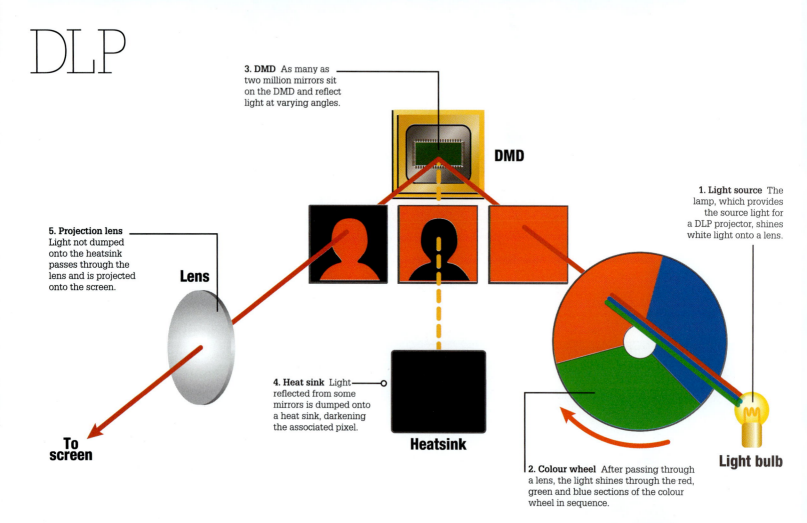

3. DMD As many as two million mirrors sit on the DMD and reflect light at varying angles.

DMD

1. Light source The lamp, which provides the source light for a DLP projector, shines white light onto a lens.

5. Projection lens Light not dumped onto the heatsink passes through the lens and is projected onto the screen.

Lens

4. Heat sink Light reflected from some mirrors is dumped onto a heat sink, darkening the associated pixel.

Heatsink

To screen

2. Colour wheel After passing through a lens, the light shines through the red, green and blue sections of the colour wheel in sequence.

Light bulb

DLP projectors work by shining a light onto a chip known as a Digital Micromirror Device (DMD). The DMD holds up to two million tiny mirrors, which tilt either towards or away from the light source up to 5000 times a second. The degree to which any given mirror is tilted dictates the shade of grey it reflects. The combination of the reflections from each mirror creates a detailed greyscale image.

Colour images are created in one of two ways. In single-chip projectors, a spinning colour wheel sits between the light source and the chip; the wheel then filters red, green or blue light onto the DMD. Thus, each mirror at any given microsecond reflects red, green or blue light. Three-chip projectors have a separate chip for each colour. The white light from the projector's lamp passes through a prism, which splits it into red, green and blue, and each colour is processed on its own DMD before being combined and passed through the projector's lens. ⓖ

LCD

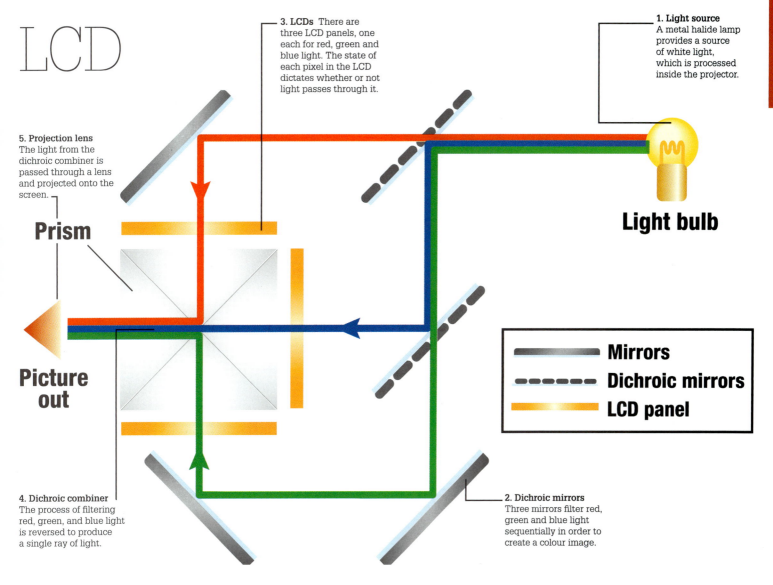

5. Projection lens
The light from the dichroic combiner is passed through a lens and projected onto the screen.

Prism

Picture out

4. Dichroic combiner
The process of filtering red, green, and blue light is reversed to produce a single ray of light.

3. LCDs There are three LCD panels, one each for red, green and blue light. The state of each pixel in the LCD dictates whether or not light passes through it.

1. Light source
A metal halide lamp provides a source of white light, which is processed inside the projector.

Light bulb

2. Dichroic mirrors
Three mirrors filter red, green and blue light sequentially in order to create a colour image.

▬▬▬ ▬▬▬	**Mirrors**
▬ ▬ ▬ ▬ ▬	**Dichroic mirrors**
▬▬▬▬▬	**LCD panel**

LCD projectors work in a similar way to LCD televisions (see p24), but instead of splitting each pixel into red, green and blue subpixels there are three separate panels to filter each colour. As light from the projector's metal halide lamp passes through each panel, pixels are switched on or off to either allow light to pass or filter it out. The light that passes through each panel is then passed through the projector's lens to produce the image onscreen.

The metal halide lamp used in LCD projectors is capable of producing a great deal of light from a very small area, so LCD projectors tend to be both brighter and more compact than DLP devices. You may hear the term "dichroic" being used in relation to LCD projectors: the dichroic mirrors split the light into red, green and blue; the dichroic combiner reverses the process. ⓘ

THE ONLY PHOTOGRAPHY BOOK
YOU'LL EVER NEED TO BUY

THE ULTIMATE GUIDE TO

DIGITAL PHOTOGRAPHY

PACKED WITH EXPERT TIPS AND TECHNIQUES

2ND EDITION

WHAT YOU NEED
Which type of camera and why

HOW TO DO IT
Software & hardware explained

TAKE STUNNING PHOTOS
Hundreds of tips and techniques

NEW EDITION UPDATED & EXPANDED

LEARN NEW DIGITAL SKILLS
▶ Photo software secrets revealed

ENHANCE YOUR SHOTS

MAKE THE MOST OF YOUR CAMERA

RETOUCH WITH EASE

ON SALE NOW

To order direct call
0844 844 0053 or visit
www.pcpro.co.uk/digphoto

JUST
£7.99
+ FREE P

Ensuring it all works together

Before you rush out and buy your brand-new set, make sure you don't make orphans of your existing standard-definition kit

As lovely as it is to embrace the brave new world of high definition, it's likely you'll be wanting to keep hold of a few standard-definition devices, too. This might include old games consoles, an existing DVD player or a video recorder. Similarly, it's worth planning what you might be adding to your TV over the next decade. Who knows what will turn up next?

So, before you throw out your trusty old TV and replace it with a new high-definition model, think about what's already plugged into it, and take a look round the back to see if you can take advantage of a better-quality output. You'll find component out (*see p38*) connectors on many DVD players, and consoles like the original Xbox and PlayStation can be fitted with component cables. Failing that, use RGB scart (as opposed to composite scart) or S-Video outputs – it will be a huge improvement over other connections.

Keeping up the standards
Most HDTVs still come equipped with sufficient standard-definition interfaces to suit your needs – often two or three scart sockets and a handy composite/S-Video at the side or front for easy access. Since you're likely to only be adding high-definition sources in the future, you shouldn't need any more than that.

Remember that standard-definition pictures may actually end up looking worse than they did on your old TV, so don't underestimate your potential desire to replace everything with HD sources sooner rather than later.

So where you could soon find your new TV lets you down is on HD inputs. Some still come with only one HDMI and one component video input, and average sets only go as far as two HDMI ports and a single component. Better examples, however, will have up to four.

Know your rights
It's also important to consider DRM (digital rights management) when it comes to future purchases. At the moment, most devices will happily work over either an HDMI or component video connection. However, copyright protection built into devices such as Blu-ray players could in the future render unprotected interfaces, such as component video, useless for outputting HD material. As a result, you should be looking to connect every device via HDMI wherever possible. Ⓖ

If you can, get a TV with Freeview built in. If yours hasn't, it's worth hooking up an external box via RGB scart, component or HDMI for best results.

Your existing DVD player will also benefit from a component or RGB scart connection if you have one. If you're also getting a Blu-ray player, you should be able to use that to play back DVDs at an upscaled resolution, in which case account for another HDMI – many won't support HD over composite.

A VCR only really needs an RGB or even composite scart connection – it's unlikely it will benefit from anything more, although some may offer S-Video or even component outputs.

If Sky or Virgin Media will be making up a large proportion of your HD content, it's worth giving it the main HDMI connection on your set.

Most Blu-ray drives currently work with both HDMI and component video connections. But in the future, discs could be restricted to HDMI only, so it's best to find them a spare connection if you can.

If you have an HDMI port going spare, it could be used by a PlayStation 3 or Xbox 360 Elite. But you won't lose much quality by using component video instead.

> ❝ **You should be looking to connect every device via HDMI wherever possible** ❞

31

CHAPTER **3** Buying

N ow you know what type of TV you're after, don't be put off by all those long lists of specifications. We'll be looking behind all the whizz-bang marketing and impressive numbers, and revealing what you really need to be looking for, what questions to ask in the shop, and which features you can safely do without. If you don't know your composite from your component, or why you need to look out for HDCP, this is the place to come. Then, to get you started, we'll look at some of the leading models and find out exactly what makes them so good.

What features do I need?

Every TV has a bewildering array of features and specifications. Learning which are important is key to finding the right one for you

The main specifications you'll see relate to the screen resolution and brightness

You'll also find features that refer to processing technologies inside the panel itself

Most of the more acronym-ridden features refer to a panel's inputs – these shouldn't be ignored

All these logos may look daunting, but some are more meaningful than others

O nce you've chosen the size of TV you want and the technology that best suits your needs, you'd be forgiven for thinking that all you need do now is pop down to your local electronics retailer and pick up a set. But when you get there, any shop worth its salt will have a wide selection of sets, each with its own seemingly random set of specifications.

There's a near-endless list of jargon to come to terms before you're able to make the right decision when buying an HDTV. It isn't helped that sales people often don't understand the terminology themselves, and repeat numbers, figures and technology blindly, hoping to make you buy the most expensive model on offer.

Jargon busting
The terms you see listed are broadly split into two groups: common specifications that you'll find listed for all televisions, and manufacturer-specific terms to describe technologies found only on that brand of TV. The first group includes common features such as brightness, contrast ratio and the type of TV tuner. These specifications can be easily compared across televisions.

The latter group has specifications specific to each manufacturer, including fancy-sounding technology like Pixel Plus or Crystal Black. These specifications can't be

compared between manufacturers, or even televisions within their ranges. The reason for this is that companies are constantly looking for new ways to differentiate their products in a very competitive market from an increasing range of very cheap but basic televisions. These technologies are all designed, with varying degrees of effectiveness, to lift picture quality above the basic sets.

Take it easy
Before you buy then, sit back, have a hot beverage of your choice, and don't be intimidated by the figures and names. The technology isn't that difficult to understand, and it's fairly straightforward to come up with a list of specifications for a TV that will suit your needs. Over the next few pages, we'll take you through all of the terms you're likely to come across, explain what they actually mean and how they work. We'll also cover some of the more common manufacturer-specific technologies, so they don't come as a surprise when you encounter them.

Take a look at the table opposite for the minimum specifications you should accept for LCD or plasma screens. This should give you a good baseline for your shortlist. Armed with a decent understanding of these features, you can stroll into the shop (or onto a website) with confidence and, ultimately, get the TV you want. ⓖ

Common features of HD

From contrast ratios to response times, proprietary pixel processing to TV tuners, we explain what you should be looking out for

Technology	LCD	Plasma
Contrast ratio	700:1+	3000:1+
Dynamic contrast ratio	Optional	Optional
Brightness	450cd/m²+	700cd/m²+
TV tuner	Digital	Digital
CI slot	Optional	Optional
Response time	16ms	N/A
100Hz	Optional	Optional
24P	Optional	Optional
Proprietary pixel processing	Optional	Optional

Minimum specs: this table shows the minimum specs we'd look for.

Contrasting opinions

One of the most important features to look for is a television's contrast ratio. This figure tells you the ratio, such as 700:1, between the darkest colour (black) and the lightest colour (white) that a TV can produce.

The contrast ratio effectively defines the range of shades a TV can produce and, therefore, how much light-and-dark detail (or contrast) you'll be able to see in the picture. Ideally, you want a TV with a high contrast ratio (a big as possible number before the ':1'), as this tells you it can produce dark blacks and bright whites simultaneously.

A low contrast ratio means blacks will tend to look slightly grey or, if you adjust the TV's settings down to get a better black, you'll get dirty greyish-whites at the other end. Low contrast ratios can make viewing some scenes difficult. For example, if you're watching something like the *Lord of the Rings* trilogy, a TV with a low contrast ratio will have trouble with the many darker, more atmospheric scenes, and you'll lose the definition you bought an HDTV for in the first place.

LCDs typically have lower contrast ratios (starting at around 700:1) than plasma screens (around 1000:1 upwards), as their constant backlight inevitably bleeds through, making their lowest black levels tending more towards the grey. However, TV manufacturers are free to use any method they like to measure the figures they quote,

so take the numbers as a guide only and, wherever possible, view a TV for yourself – check you're happy with the depth of its blacks and the purity of its whites, and where possible compare it with the competition.

Be dynamic

You'll notice that some LCD televisions will have a very high contrast ratio, but look out for a specification named something like 'dynamic contrast ratio'. The figure quoted here isn't the screen's true contrast ratio, but rather the result of some clever technology inside.

This works by monitoring the input and adjusting the backlight of the screen accordingly to increase the contrast ratio. Very dark scenes cause the backlight to be lowered, increasing the number of dark shades that can be displayed and making blacks blacker; very light scenes cause the backlight to be increased, raising the number of light shades that can be displayed and making whites whiter.

Dynamic contrast ratios work brilliantly for certain types of scenes. Movies and games typically have scenes with low dynamic ranges (the range between the dark and light colours), so adjusting the backlight can really bring out detail and make a massive difference. However, for scenes with extremes of both, the backlight can't be adjusted to compensate. In this case, you're stuck with the TV's

"While specifications can tell you a lot, there's nothing better than seeing a television in action..."

standard contrast ratio. Sets with dynamic contrast ratios will display a better picture for much of the time, but try to find out the standard contrast ratio too, so you get an idea of how well the TV will perform in all circumstances.

Bright eyes

The brightness of a TV is measured in candelas per square metre (cd/m^2). There's no need to understand exactly what this measurement means (suffice to say candles are involved), only that the higher the number, the brighter the picture. A brighter picture looks more natural and will cope better under stronger lighting conditions. A darker TV means you'll need to dim the lights or even draw the curtains to get the best picture. As a rough guide, even the cheapest TV has a $400cd/m^2$ brightness, which is enough for most rooms. $600cd/m^2$ or brighter televisions should be fine in all but direct sunlight.

TV tuners

Once the UK's analogue signal has been turned off (see p16), analogue tuners won't pick up anything but static. The only way to receive standard television channels will be then be with a digital Freeview or Freesat receiver – either in your television or through a separate set-top box. Practically every TV sold now will come with an integrated Freeview tuner (and a handful also come with Freesat), so you don't have to face the hassle or expense of getting a set-top box for the immediate future.

CI, CAM, USB and memory card slots

If you want extra channels, a Common Interface (CI) slot can be useful. This takes a Conditional Access Module (CAM) – or viewing card – granting access to premium content such as Setanta Sports (*www.setantasports.com*). It's slim pickings at the moment, although this could change when analogue TV is turned off. So while it's a nice feature, a CI slot is far from essential.

Many sets also now come with USB slots or SD card readers, allowing you to watch video clips, view photos, or even listen to MP3s directly from the TV. If that's something you'd find handy, go for it. But bear in mind that many other input devices (such as games consoles and DVD players) do the same, often in a much more convenient way.

100Hz

One of the traditional issues with TV is that the relatively low frame rate can lead to ghosting or motion blur, particularly on fast-moving scenes. 100Hz sets aim to cut this out by doubling the frame rate of television from 50fps (standard 50Hz sets) to 100fps - with a handful of top-end sets now even going up to 200Hz. This is achieved by the TV introducing an 'averaged' artificial frame between two real frames. The idea is that this creates a smoother flow and should eliminate ghosting. And while it's effective when done well, the effect can be quite subtle if you're not looking for it. The best way to check this is to view the TV in store yourself – horizontal scrolling text is the best test for it.

24P

That set frame rate – 50fps in the UK – also causes problems for cinefilm (filmed at 24fps), as this information has to be matched to the TV's frame rate. This is achieved

by actually speeding up the film slightly, or on US transfers (where the frame rate is 60fps) dropping every third frame. Either way, the net effect is that you're no longer left with quite what the film maker intended and, as with any processing, errors can be introduced.

TVs with 24P (also called a 24fps mode) can run natively at 24fps, the same as films. In this mode, there's no alteration to an input signal and you get exactly what the film maker intended. While that's great, it's a nice-to-have feature that tends to mark out more expensive sets, and we'd only recommend it as essential for the well-heeled film buff.

Response time

All LCD screens all have a delay in adjusting the colour of their pixels, as a matrix of crystals has to physically twist into a new shape. This measurement is expressed as 'response time': the number of milliseconds a monitor takes to change a pixel from active to inactive and back. The lower the number, the faster the TV can switch, meaning the screen updates more quickly, and motion theoretically appears more smoothly and without smeary ghosting. A minimum of 16ms is recommended, but if you can get 8ms or faster, even better. Response times are sometimes listed as 'grey-to-grey', which is quicker to perform, but incomparable with the true speeds. Typically, if you can't find the 'true' value, adding 4ms to the grey-to-grey time should give a reasonable estimate.

Proprietary techniques

Spend much time looking at TV specs, and you'll soon come across fancy-sounding marketing terms such as Pixel Plus on Philips TVs or Bravia Engine on Sony sets. These terms refer to proprietary pixel-processing technologies, generally unique to a specific manufacturer. But while they're impossible to compare directly, they shouldn't be ignored, as this extra level of electronics can be very important.

For starters, standard-definition footage (such as Freeview or DVDs) has to be upscaled to be viewed at a TV's native resolution. Simply put, more advanced pixel-processing technology can make this look more natural. Pixel processing can also help produce more vibrant pictures, smoother motion and reduce stutter, ghosting and noise – particularly on LCD sets.

Making your choice

The table on the previous page gives you the minimum figures you should look for in a TV (LCD and plasma), but try to get better where you can. And remember that while specifications can certainly tell you a lot, there's nothing better than seeing a television in action for yourself, so we recommend visiting a showroom, even if you're intending to do some bargain hunting online.

Take along a favourite DVD (or even better, a Blu-ray disc) and ask to view it on the TVs you're interested in. You'll then get a true idea of how it performs. If they won't let you, go somewhere else. This is better than trusting the display footage in the shop – either picked to make the TVs look their best or, worse, from a crummy aerial on the roof.

So don't get sucked in by the sales patter or impressively high numbers: get even a basic grasp on the technical terms and you have a better chance of ending up with a TV that suits you, not the salesman's targets. ⓖ

Video and audio connections

Know your HDMI from your DVI? Or your composite video from your S-Video? What about coax digital audio and optical digital audio...? Help is at hand...

→ HDMI

HDMI (High-Definition Multimedia Interface) is the digital equivalent of scart – it's a single cable connection that can carry both audio and video signals. HDMI can carry HD video signals up to the current maximum resolution of 1080p and also supports HDCP, which allows protected content to be viewed. HDMI is backwards compatible with DVI, so you can easily convert between the two – for example, to view the DVI output of a PC on your HDTV.

→ DVI

DVI (Digital Visual Interface) is a digital video connection commonly used by PCs and early HD televisions. DVI can carry both digital and analogue signals, but not audio data. DVI also supports HDCP, so can be used to transfer protected content. And it's compatible with HDMI video signals, so can be easily converted using an adapter. The DVI-D variant only carries digital signals, but the more common DVI-I will carry analogue signals, too.

HDCP

HDCP (High-bandwidth Digital Content Protection) was developed by Intel to stop content being copied.

HDCP requires all devices in a chain to be trusted, including the parts within devices. A PC's Blu-ray drive, for example, needs an HDCP-compliant graphics card too, or content won't be digitally output at full resolution.

All data is encrypted, with each device needing a key to work with other HDCP devices. Keys can also be revoked, so if a device is found to be insecure, the key can be invalidated. Should this happen, the device won't work with new versions of HDCP equipment.

Blu-ray players also include ICT (Image Constraint Token), allowing content owners to specify what happens when using unprotected outputs such as component or VGA. If the ICT is turned on, then the output may be downscaled to a much reduced 960 x 540 pixels, or even blocked entirely.

We've yet to see the ICT flag used in anger (just as well given that earlier HD devices don't have HDMI or DVI), but this looks set to change soon. As such, it's all the more reason to use an HDMI connection.

→ VGA

VGA (Video Graphics Array) is an analogue video connection commonly used on PCs, although it's largely been replaced by DVI. Many HDTVs have VGA connectors for PC input rather than DVI, though, and it's also commonly seen on projectors. Some games consoles can also output in VGA with a converter cable. However, it's always preferable to use a digital signal where possible. Cheap adapters are available to convert from DVI to VGA.

→ COMPONENT VIDEO

Component video is an analogue connection standard that supports high-definition signals. It uses three RCA connectors, usually red, blue and green (and labelled PR, PB and Y). Component video is capable of supporting HD resolutions up to 1080p and, as it uses three cables to transfer the video information, it's less susceptible to interference. It doesn't, however, carry HDCP information, so HDMI remains preferable (*see left*).

→ 5.1 CHANNEL ANALOGUE AUDIO

5.1 channel audio uses RCA cables to transfer a decoded surround-sound signal. Unlike a digital connection, which only requires a single wire, analogue 5.1 channel audio needs six separate cables to transfer the audio information for the left, right, centre, rear left, rear right and subwoofer signals that make up a surround system.

→ STEREO RCA AND MINI-JACK

Analogue stereo audio requires at least three wires – one each for left and right and a common ground cable. It's common to see both two RCA sockets (one for each channel) or a single mini-jack socket (such as a headphone connector) on equipment, and it's easy to convert between the two with an adapter cable.

→ SCART

Scart (Syndicat des Constructeurs d'Appareils Radiorécepteurs et Téléviseurs, to you) is a 21-pin analogue video and audio connector commonly seen on video equipment sold in Europe. Scart connections can support RGB, S-Video or composite video signals, as well as stereo audio. Scart cables can also send signalling information, to tell a TV to switch from 4:3 to widescreen, for example. RGB is the best quality variant.

→ S-VIDEO

S-Video is an analogue, non-HD video connection that splits the video signal into separate chrominance and luminance signals, making it a better-quality option than composite, which lumps all the signals together, suffering interference as a result. S-Video is a round connector with four pins, commonly seen on camcorders and usually on the front or side of TVs for easy access. There's also a 7-pin variant, which is typically found on higher-end kit.

→ COAX DIGITAL AUDIO

Coax digital audio is similar to optical digital audio, except that it uses a coaxial cable with RCA connectors to transmit the digital audio information. Although it's possible to translate between optical and coax digital connections, converters are relatively expensive, so it's always worth checking which digital audio connection is supported before buying home cinema equipment.

→ COMPOSITE VIDEO

Composite video is the lowest-quality connection in use and should be avoided wherever possible. As it only uses a single RCA connector to carry the video signal, it suffers from significant interference and poor image quality. When compared with other video sources, the inferiority of composite is especially apparent when viewed on an HD set. You'll also notice that composite cables are often pretty ropey too. Note that it also comes in a scart form.

→ RF AERIAL

RF Aerial was originally an analogue-only connection used to transmit 'terrestrial' broadcast channels. It's now also used to carry digital broadcasts on Freeview, allowing significantly more channels to be broadcast digitally in the same amount of space as a single analogue channel – albeit still currently at standard definition. Be careful of cheap cables or extensions, as a poor interface will significantly degrade signal quality.

PRICES

Take a look at the prices for some of these cables and you could be in for a shock – a single HDMI cable can cost hundreds of pounds. But while better-quality cables will yield better results, don't go too crazy unless everything else is the very top of the range. As we explore in more depth on p112, it's generally worth replacing bundled cables, though, as these are usually poor quality.

→ OPTICAL DIGITAL AUDIO

Optical digital cables use fibre optics to transfer audio information digitally. The signal can be encoded in a surround-sound format such as Dolby Digital or DTS (*see p114*), or just be raw PCM (pulse-code modulation) information. In order to benefit from surround-sound formats, you'll need an amplifier or AV receiver (*see p105*) with a built-in decoder to process it.

LCD TVs

With a huge number of LCD TVs vying for your attention, we pick out six of the very best

➔ PHILIPS 42PFL9703D

Price:	£1800
Internet:	www.philips.co.uk
Rating:	★★★★★

This is a very pricey TV – but boy, does it have its reasons. For starters, the design is gorgeous, with a sleek frontage and superb build quality. Then there's the unique Ambilight Spectra 3, which groovily throws out coloured light from the left, right and top edges in sympathy with images. These are pretty special too, with a vast list of picture processing collectively called Perfect Pixel HD: 100Hz processing, motion smoothing, superb upscaling tricks and numerous elements for improving colour saturations and tones.

   Spend time calibrating it, and you'll get some of the best detail, sharpness, colour richness, brightness and fluidity to be found on any LCD TV. All that processing does cause the occasional artefact, but that's minor in the context of the good it does for both standard and high definition sources. Despite a slick menu system, the sheer number of options also potentially make it complicated to use – but the rewards are immense.

➔ LG 47LG7000

Price:	£1400
Internet:	www.lge.co.uk
Rating:	★★★★★

Obvious gimmicks on a TV often point to a rat. And this set's unique wireless Bluetooth feature, which lets you transfer mobile phone pictures to the TV, or listen to it via wireless headphones, certainly falls into the nice-but-pointless camp. But the real interest lies elsewhere. Behind the attractive – if slightly chunky – bodywork you'll find four HDMI inputs, and a USB 2 input for playing JPEG and MP3 files.

   But it's the picture processing that's the star, with a 100Hz mode with the 'TruMotion' system for more fluid (if not flawless) motion; and LG's XD Engine system, which boosts colours, contrast and detail. Colours look natural, motion clean and black levels are good in all but the very darkest scenes. Standard definition also survives the journey up to the full HD resolution remarkably well. The potent sound system seals the deal. You'll find better blacks elsewhere, but the overall performance truly shines.

➔ SONY KDL-40W4000

Price:	£950
Internet:	www.sony.co.uk
Rating:	★★★★★

The good news begins with the Sony's looks: robust 'Midnight Sky' (AKA black) bezel, sumptuously offset by a silver metallic trim and novel see-through bottom edge. Three HDMIs, a PC input, and a USB input tick the right boxes, with a PhotoTV HD mode that optimises settings to suit stills, and a Picture Frame mode that reduces power usage by 35%.

   But the most important feature is the Bravia Engine 2 processing, which works wonders on both high and especially standard definition pictures. Motion handling is excellent, leaving you free to appreciate the wondrous detail and sharpness in HD pictures, and the impressive clarity of standard definition sources. Colours are vivid yet natural, and black levels are detailed, if occasionally just a touch noisy. 100Hz processing would be nice, but with robust sonics keeping the mostly sublime pictures company, this is about as good as LCD TVs get.

➲ SAMSUNG LE40A656

Price:	£840
Internet:	www.samsung.co.uk
Rating:	★★★★★

40IN

This truly gorgeous TV stands out for two reasons. Initially, it's the black bezel infused strikingly with hint of red, but this is also the first TV built without rivets or glue in the outer bodywork, giving a glorious seamless finish. Nice. It also stands out by providing four HDMI inputs, as well as a USB input for JPEG pictures and MP3 audio files. Its full HD resolution is joined by a high 50000:1 claimed contrast ratio and 100Hz processing, leaving pictures more or less free of motion blur and judder.

Detail levels are terrific with HD, inky blacks mix with gleaming whites. and ultra-vivid colour tones there's a and sense of dynamism you just don't get in this price bracket. Standard definition sources are upscaled with aplomb too. The factory settings are over-aggressive (so change them), and the speakers are slightly feeble, but the stunning design, gorgeous pictures and aggressive price make this set the very definition of desirable.

➲ PANASONIC TX-32LZD85

Price:	£700
Internet:	www.panasonic.co.uk
Rating:	★★★★☆

32IN

Despite being a staunch plasma advocate, Panasonic also knows its way round LCD technology too. There's a full HD resolution for a start – far from a given on a 32in set. There's a 100Hz mode for clear motion reproduction, Motion Focus, which optimises the backlight to the picture, and a dynamic contrast range of 10000:1.The redoubtable V-Real picture processing system reduces video noise, enhances detail, boosts colours and improves contrast levels.

It's pretty easy on the eye, too, while connections include three HDMIs, a PC port and an SD card slot. Where it really shines, though, is the quality of its pictures in both SD and HD, with bright, cheerful, solidly saturated colours and some of the very best black levels across the board. In fact, the only serious negative note we have is some occasional flickering from the 100Hz processing. But otherwise it's all good. Very good.

➲ TOSHIBA 37CV505DB

Price:	£600
Internet:	www.toshiba.co.uk
Rating:	★★★★☆

37IN

No, we haven't made a mistake – this is a £600 HD ready 37in LCD TV. Admittedly, first impressions aren't promising, with little design subtlety and more than a bit of plastic. But it soon starts to look up: three v1.3 HDMIs are present, as is the PC port that often goes AWOL at this price level.

There's no full HD resolution, 24P or 100Hz modes, unsurprisingly, but the claimed contrast ratio of 15000:1 and Toshiba's Active Vision LCD processing are particularly eye-catching. Together, they produce pictures that, while hardly world-beaters, are certainly better than you'd expect, particularly in HD, with impressive detail and very little motion blur.

Our only real problems with the 37CV505DB are that 1080p/24 sources look slightly juddery, and standard definition pictures can look a bit noisy unless they're of a really high quality in the first place. But this doesn't stop the set from being a real bargain.

Plasma TVs

SAMSUNG PS-63P76FD

Price:	£3300
Internet:	www.samsung.co.uk
Rating:	★★★★☆

At 63in across, that's what we call a good start, with a full HD pixel count, a contrast ratio of 16000:1 and a franky silly claimed colour response of 18 quadrillion different hues. Impressive numbers are reinforced by three v1.3 HDMI ports, plus a good range of other inputs. Full use is made of its resolution, oozing sharpness and detail, plus exceptional colour handling, richness, contrast and brightness. There's also an extra punch given by a general brightness level that's unusual by big-screen plasma standards.

It's not utterly perfect, with the Movie Plus processing mode causing the occasional flickering artefact when dealing with really rapid movement; dark areas can look a touch green; and some skin tones and deep reds can look slightly unnatural. But so far as we're concerned these seem pretty small prices to pay for the sheer size and overall quality of the PS63P76FD's truly cinema-sized pictures.

PIONEER PDP-LX5090

Price:	£2700
Internet:	www.pioneer.co.uk
Rating:	★★★★★

The KURO series revolutionised our expectations of what flat-panel TVs can do, with incredible inky blacks and tremendous all-round performance. And this second-generation model is spectacularly good. It removes practically all trace of the greyness over dark areas that plagues every other flat TV to some extent. Its colours are also fearsomely intense and natural by plasma standards, HD pictures look phenomenally sharp on the LX5090's full HD screen too, motion is handled pretty much immaculately, and noise of every sort is supremely well suppressed, even when watching standard definition.

As if its peerless pictures weren't attraction enough, the LX5090 also looks very tasty, sounds great through its powerful, detachable speakers and is well connected thanks to three HDMIs and a USB port. Aside from a slightly overcomplicated setup, it's about as perfect a TV as you'll find. The only problem is finding someone to buy your kidneys so you can afford one.

PANASONIC TH-46PZ81

Price:	£1400
Internet:	www.panasonic.co.uk
Rating:	★★★★★

At long last, Sky has a satellite broadcasting rival, and this is one of a handful of sets with a Freesat (as well as a Freeview and analogue) tuner built in, removing the need for a separate receiver box. And with a number of channels on Freeview that aren't on Freesat, it's worth using both.

As you'd hope, it'll receive Freesat's HD channels, BBC HD and ITV HD, using its full HD 1920 x 1080 pixel count to full effect. It also does a neat job of organising all the extensive Freesat and Freeview channel information into excellent electronic programme guides. There's plenty of picture processing technology to help SD broadcasts look as good as possible. They work together to ensure extremely impressive pictures, with Freesat HD broadcasts particularly fine, unusually good upscaling skills and expressive, clean audio. In all, it's both a mighty fine TV as well as just the sort of premium partner the Freesat service really needs right now.

➡ HITACHI P50XR01

Price:	£1400
Internet:	www.hitachi.co.uk
Rating:	★★★★☆

Fancy a fully functioning Freeview HDD PVR system inside an all-singing, all-dancing 50in plasma TV? Well, here you go. There's also a full HD native resolution, SD and USB ports for direct playback of JPEGs, a PC port, three v1.3 HDMIs and some significant processing, including Hitachi's Frame Rate Conversion and Picture Master, which covers 24P support and seom very impressive colour and noise reduction technologies.

The recording section comprises a 250GB hard disk for 100 hours or so of programmes. The only pity is that it doesn't support Series Link. Its near-flawless recording quality isn't quite reinforced by the pictures from its screen, with murky black levels and some slightly off-key colours. But there's plenty of good news, with stunningly crisp, clean pictures and smooth movement handling. With its unique features at this size, not to mention an attractive price, it's easy to overlook its shortcomings.

➡ LG 50PG6000

Price:	£900
Internet:	www.lge.co.uk
Rating:	★★★★☆

This TV wears its heart on its price ticket: 50in of plasma for just £900. But that's not its only party trick, with great looks and sensuously arced silver power light. Connections are easily up to speed too, with three HDMIs, a PC port, plus a USB socket for JPEG stills and MP3 audio files. With a contrast ratio claim of 30000:1, 100Hz processing and full 1080p/24fps Blu-ray support, only the 1366 x 768 resolution gives the game away. But it doesn't stop some startlingly detailed performance.

Black levels may not be the deepest, but they outgun the majority of LCDs, with dark movie scenes highly convincing. Colours impress too, combining decent levels of brightness with reasonably natural tones, while the 100Hz processing helps smooth out moving objects. Standard definition pictures look slightly rough versus the best, but in the context of its £900 asking price, the 50PG6000 is such good value it's almost silly.

➡ PANASONIC TH-42PX80

Price:	£640
Internet:	www.panasonic.co.uk
Rating:	★★★★★

We're still amazed that you can get this much TV for this little money – and with a robust build and understated elegance, no-one need know, either. Three HDMI inputs, a PC port and, for digital photo playback, an SD card slot are a good start too. Don't be put off by the HD ready 1024 x 768 resolution either, as the V-Real 3 processing does a cracking job at delivering sharp, clean and natural pictures. It also does unusually well at upscaling standard definition sources too, But the real the star attraction is black level response, with dark scenes looking cinematic, three-dimensional and dynamic in a way that just shouldn't happen at this price.

In an ideal world, the colour response would be slightly more vibrant, certain hues could be more natural, and a full HD resolution would be just a touch sharper. But these really are minor gripes when you consider the competition at this price level. If you're after a bargain 42in set, this is it.

Other HD devices

➲ APPLE IMAC

Price	From £799
Internet	www.apple.com/uk
Rating	★★★★☆

With some stunning looks and slick marketing, many people don't need to know much more to buy an Apple iMac. The all-in-one design nonchalantly hides away all of the computer paraphernalia, including a fast dual-core processor and 802.11n wireless networking – you can basically just plug it in and go.

You just have to decide how high a specification you need and how big a screen you can afford: the sumptuous 24in version offers a more-than-full HD 1920 x 1200 resolution.

Apple's Front Row media centre software oozes style, too, with an interface that makes the majority of its competitors look distinctly 20th century. You can access all of your iTunes files using Apple's tidy remote, and download HD video and TV shows from the iTunes store with ease, as well as view photos on the bright and crisp TFT screen.

Unfortunately, that's where the HD party comes to a halt, as there's no option for built-in Blu-ray, and while you could hook up an external drive if you really want to, it will add a big chunk to the price. While the iMac actually has the common HD codecs built in to the OS X operating system, the lack of HD hardware remains a problem – although the top end models will handle some HD gaming. We're sure Apple will step up to the HD mark in style soon, but it's not quite ready to replace all your other kit as yet.

➲ HP TOUCHSMART IQ800

Price	Around £1500
Internet	www.hp.com/uk
Rating	★★★★☆

Back in the eighties, it seemed obvious that the near future would be full of touchscreens, but it's only now that they're beginning to have any kind of impact. And the TouchSmart series from HP is testament to how good this new kind of future can be.

With a serious 25.5in screen running at 1900 x 1200 pixels, it's more than full HD resolution, and comes with a slot-loading Blu-ray drive neatly hidden in the side, so you make the most of it. 802.11n Wi-Fi also means you can wirelessly stream media to it from other computers (see p120), or browse the internet at lightning speeds.

It makes use of HP's bespoke TouchSmart software, which runs on top of Windows Vista, and makes most jobs instantly finger-friendly. Choosing photos, managing music playlists or web browsing can all be done without visiting the Windows desktop.

The sturdy stand and sleek design (including some nifty mood lighting) make it equally suited to the study, kitchen or bedroom, making it ideal for those looking for a versatile second HD system, particularly as it's wall mountable, comes with a TV tuner built in, and very capable Nvidia 9600M graphics card to cope with some gaming. Add in the webcam, excellent wireless keyboard and mouse, and it's the most impressive touchscreen PC yet to appear.

MEDIA-CENTRE PC

DELL STUDIO HYBRID
£770
www.dell.co.uk

★★★★☆

The Studio Hybrid is a media PC with a difference. Measuring just 20 x 21 x 7cm, it'll nestle unobtrusively next to a big-screen HDTV, but its tiny oval form conceals a fully fledged, Blu-ray-equipped computer.

It certainly helps that it's so devilishly attractive too. The supplied stand allows it to be stood vertically or horizontally, and the combination of smooth, glossy curves and gently glowing logos make for a preternaturally good looking package. If the standard Slate Grey shell doesn't excite, you can choose from a range of five different colours (a second choice comes as

standard), including a rather nice Bamboo shell – though this has a hefty £90 premium attached.

It doesn't rival full-sized PCs for sheer power or upgradeability, but it's still supremely capable. Thanks to the use of components more often found in the cramped confines of a laptop, noise is kept to virtually inaudible levels too, while the Intel Core 2 Duo processor and accompanying 3GB of memory keep Windows Vista running happily on the capacious 320GB hard drive, which gives plenty of room for music and photos.

There's an HD decoder card built in, keeping hi-def movies jerk and judder-free, while the HDMI socket at the rear ferries pristine 1080p images to your HDTV or projector of choice. Only the omission of a built-in digital TV tuner disappoints, but add the likes of Terratec's superb Cinergy DT USB diversity XS to one of the rear-ward facing USB ports, and you'll have a pint-sized media centre PC that looks as good as all that HD content.

➔ ACER ASPIRE 8930G

Price	Around £1500
Internet	www.acer.co.uk
Rating	★★★★★

Acer's Aspire Gemstone Blue range was one of the first to embrace movie-friendly 16:9 displays and this, the flagship model is one of the best entertainment laptops around.

The generous 18.4in screen boasts a full-HD 1920 x 1080 resolution, and the glossy finish imbues images with tremendous vibrance. Blu-ray movies are rendered with stunning detail, but the superb image quality also makes the best of standard definition sources such as DVD, or TV via the inbuilt Freeview tuner. The array of touch-sensitive sensitive buttons to the left of the comfy full-sized keyboard, makes light work of navigating around too.

It's also unusually blessed with a superb set of five speakers and a subwoofer, scattered around the sizable frame, and making an impressively bombastic fist of movie soundtracks. It's not enough to rival separate 5.1 sets, but it's the most immersive performance we've heard from integrated laptop speakers.

The 4.2kg weight and modest battery life means that you won't be watching Blu-ray on the move, but 802.11n Wi-Fi will keep you closer to your media than ever before.

It all comes at a substantial price, but the Acer is a true do-it-all laptop. There's power in spades thanks to Intel Centrino 2 hardware, and the latest Nvidia integrated graphics ensures that HD gaming is on the agenda too.

➔ SONY VAIO VGN-FW11ZU

Price	£1180
Internet	www.dell.co.uk
Rating	★★★★☆

This laptop crams high performance HD hardware into a chic chassis. From the moment you tilt back its sturdy, sizable lid, its fine media credentials are designed to impress. The glossy 16.4in display strikes a good middle ground between traditional 15.4in and 17in models, but still allows it to hit a happily portable 2.9kg on the scales.

In a move away from the 16:10 ratio displays found on other laptops, the glossy panel adopts a movie-friendly 16:9 ratio. That means fewer black bars at the top and bottom of the screen, and the image quality is sublime. Sony's dual-lamp technology gives outstanding brightness, superb contrast and excellent colour reproduction, making for a superb movie experience. The 1600 x 900 native resolution may sound disappointing, but it barely matters on such a compact display. Blu-ray movies are rendered with striking vibrancy, and fine detail is beyond reproach.

The built-in Blu-ray drive will also write discs, and the specification is more than powerful enough to take HD video editing in its stride. With 4GB of RAM and a generous 300GB hard disk, it's enough to rival desktop PCs, and with ATI's Radeon Mobility 3650 chipset, plus an HDMI port for hooking up to the big-screen and 802.11n networking for lightning-fast hi-def media streaming, and the Sony offers simply stupendous value for money.

Buying checklist and tips

Don't just buy the first HDTV you see... Find out what you really need, and what features you can safely do without

Buying tips

Always get a demo Our golden rule: even if you're planning to buy online, try visiting a showroom to see your model in action. Don't just take their word for it, either: TVs are often tweaked in-store to look their brightest, but surprisingly few will actually be showing HD content.

Take your time You're likely to be spending some serious money, so don't be hurried. A dealer worth their salt will let you try out suitable content (such as a familiar film) on a couple of sets in your own time. Check ahead of time and, if they don't sound keen, go somewhere else. Check both SD and HD performance while you're at it and, if possible, the performance of the built-in tuners.

Plasma or LCD? While you need to be aware of the shortcomings of each, don't get too hung up on one or the other. Let your eyes be the judge, and go for the model that suits your size and budget requirements.

1080p? Purists will inevitably say yes, but, again, don't get too stuck on the question – it's ultimately your eyes, not the specs that will judge the picture. A merely average 1080p panel won't look as good as a great 720p model.

Picture processing? You'll pay extra for the best. Bear in mind that it will affect SD and HD pictures in different ways, so take a look at both types for yourself where possible.

Check prices first If buying in person, look at online prices *before* you head out to the shops. You might find you can make some savings online, although not always.

Check model numbers Even a single missing letter or extra digit can mean a totally different panel or, at the very least, a different colour than you were expecting. If you see a TV much cheaper than anywhere else, make sure it's really the one you're after.

More HDMI is better Having just a single HDMI port now may not seem a problem, but if there's one feature you should overshoot on it's this. Aim for at least two, with three or four being ideal.

Don't get features you won't use If you know you're going to get HD cable or satellite, is the CAM slot essential? And if you're going to supply your own speakers don't fret about the quality of those that come built in. Not going to look at photos on it? Then see if you can get a higher quality panel at the same price, without a USB input.

Know your limits Don't let sales people skew you from your hard-wrought decisions or price bracket – remember, you'll need to kit yourself out with more than just a TV, and wall-mounting brackets and cables don't come cheap. And consider whether the extended warranty is really worth taking – check the small print before signing.

Know your rights Check the company's return policy, especially if buying online, as it may not accept returns in the event that you simply change your mind once the screen arrives. But also make sure the panel is free of faults on delivery, as manufacturing defects should be covered by the warranty, and returns may not be accepted later.

Time to pay Use a credit card to pay if you have one – this provides extra protection in the case of transit damage or if the company goes into administration before your TV is delivered. The alternative could prove horribly costly.

HDTV Checklist

	Wanted...	Shortlisted TV 1	Shortlisted TV 2
Size range?	....	....	....
Price range?	....	....	....
HD ready or Full HD?	....	....	....
Built-in DVB-T tuner?	☐	☐	☐
Built-in analogue tuner?	☐	☐	☐
Number of scart inputs?	....	....	....
Component input?	☐	☐	☐
DVI input? HDCP?	....	....	....
S-Video input?	☐	☐	☐
Number of HDMI inputs?	....	....	....
Memory card reader?	☐	☐	☐
24p/film mode?	☐	☐	☐
100Hz?	☐	☐	☐

Now you've found the high-definition light of your life, you need to set it up. Where are you going to put it? On the wall, like you live in an advert, or on a brand-new coffee table? We provide the answers. Plus, chances are it won't look its best out of the box, so we'll also be looking at calibrating your new screen and speakers before delving into advanced tuning-up. We'll then turn our attention to getting it all working with the rest of your system, and making the best out of your Freeview signal.

Positioning and mounting

Before you simply plonk your new HDTV on that cheap old table, have a think about your options, as it could make all the difference...

Besides the joys of HD, flat-panel LCDs and plasmas have another advantage over CRT – the fact that you can mount them in a variety of places. The simplest solution for most people is to place it on top of a TV bench, with room for your DVD player and other hi-fi equipment underneath. That keeps everything tidy, negates the need for extra-long cables, and will generally place the screen at a comfortable viewing height when you're sat on a sofa. You can even buy TV benches with built-in speakers, if you're feeling flash.

Wall-mounting
A common alternative to all this is to hang your flat-panel TV on the wall, where it will protrude by only a few inches. You'll find a step-by-step guide on how to do this on p53. As long as you're comfortable with a drill and a screwdriver, and you have the budget for a decent wall bracket and longer cables, but it needn't be difficult.

The principle challenge with wall-mounting is cabling: at the very least you'll need power, plus numerous HDMI or component cables to connect your other sources. One option is to hide the cables behind the plaster, which will involve an electrician, builder and / or plasterer. Only attempt the job yourself at all if you're absolutely comfortable with what you're doing, and are sure you know where the existing lighting and power cables run – drilling into live wire could kill you. Which is no fun at all.

A cheaper, easier option is to clip the wires neatly to the wall or, better still, use trunking to hide the cables. This will still be noticeable against a flat wall, even if you paint it the same colour, so if your carpentry skills are up to it you could attempt to make a feature out of it by constructing a plinth in front to hide the cabling, while keeping everything accessible.

Position in the room
One of the primary considerations is avoiding reflections and glare wherever possible, as this could completely ruin all your hard work getting the best picture. So, naturally, you should avoid placing the HDTV where a window will be clearly visible in it as a reflection – more a problem on glass-fronted plasma screens than on LCDs, which are pretty forgiving when it comes to glare. While having some form of backlighting is actually a good idea, having a large window behind the TV isn't ideal either, since the difference in brightness isn't easily in your control and it can all too easily leave the screen washed out and cause eye-strain.

Placing may also be limited by where you'll be sitting, as it won't be particularly comfortable sitting side on. Plus, you should consider the sitting distance – hopefully you'll have factored this in before buying (*see p20*), as this will also make a difference to your perception of quality. Sit too close to a big screen, and you'll see the flaws at lower resolutions; too far and you won't appreciate the quality.

A final factor to consider is audio. If you're planning to use a surround-sound speaker set, you'll want to position the HDTV so that it's in the centre of the two or three front speakers to ensure the surround experience is as realistic as possible. Depending on how large your lounge is, you might still be able to place the TV in a corner, but most rooms will benefit from having the TV towards the centre of a wall. For a fuller guide on how to position your surround speakers, see p111.

How high?
Wherever you choose to mount the screen, make sure it's at a comfortable height. You don't want to tilt your head upwards to see the whole picture – that'll quickly lead to neck strain. Ergonomic experts recommend the middle of the screen be at eye level, although the actual height you can get away with will depend on the size and proportions of your room – as well as the height of your seating.

Some research suggests you should avoid looking too far above where the horizon would be – apparently we've evolved to associate that with danger, and you won't be able to relax. While we can't prove that conclusively, mounting a 42in HDTV up high in a narrow room certainly doesn't work as well as it does in a wider one. ⓖ

PHILIPS AMBILIGHT

All TVs will look pretty nifty mounted on the wall, but Philips' series of Ambilight TVs will look especially smart. They use a series of lights behind the bezel to backlight the wall in sympathy with what's on the screen. The flagship model – the Aurea (*shown right*) takes the concept even further, using over 150 LEDs to extend the picture across its glass bezel and onto the surrounding walls, creating a ripple of ever-changing colours. The effect is mesmerising, and surprisingly effective. It will even act as mood lighting when there's no picture displayed.

INTRO | CHOOSING | BUYING | SETTING UP | ENJOYING HD | HD ON YOUR PC | EXPANSION | HD HOME

" ...research suggests you should avoid looking too far above where the horizon would be..."

Wall-mounting your HDTV

Wall-mounting your HDTV needn't be a difficult job. All you need is a willing helper and some basic DIY skills

If you're comfortable hanging pictures and mounting shelves, and know how to use a power drill, tape measure and a stud finder, you should have no problems wall-mounting your HDTV.

Before you start, though, make sure you know the local building regulations, since they may prevent you from running power cables within walls. Also, be sure you know what's behind the wall you intend to mount the TV on before drilling or cutting into it. And, if in doubt, consult a builder.

Wall brackets

Unless your HDTV came with a wall bracket, and not many do, you'll need to buy one. Ideally, you should buy the appropriate mounting kit (mentioned in your owner's manual) from the same manufacturer. If this isn't possible, you can buy any VESA bracket that matches the mounting holes on the back of your TV – worth double-checking.

Usually, you'll see something like VESA 75 or VESA 100/200. The former means that the holes are in a square and are 75mm apart. 100/200 means they're in a 100 x 200mm rectangle. You'll find that most brackets are compatible with multiple standards and you can usually choose one that lets you tilt the screen by around 15-20 degrees in each direction. Some brackets let you adjust the height of the TV, while others allow it to tilt and swivel.

Don't skimp on the quality of a bracket, though, as you don't want your HDTV to descend at high speed to your floor – a substandard version might not be able to handle the weight. Never exceed the stated maximum weight that a bracket is rated. And avoid bargain-bin versions.

Cabling

Hiding wires isn't an easy job, but you'll need to do something to avoid the power and signal cables being an eyesore. One way to neaten things up is to get an electrician to put a power socket behind where the HDTV will hang. While they're doing this, you might also be able to get them to run HDMI and any other cables you'll need in the same channels in the wall.

Alternatively, you could opt for wireless HDMI. This is exactly what it sounds – a wireless connection between an HDMI source and an HDTV with an HDMI input. Despite being on the horizon for years, the first wireless HDMI products are only just emerging now, however, and standards have yet to be agreed. But systems from Philips and other manufacturers use ultrawideband technology to send the HD video to the receiver over distances of up to 20m. Considering the flexibility it gives you in placing your screen and HD sources, you may feel it's worth investing the £200-£300 it will cost. ⓖ

CABLING

If you're running all the cables in the wall, make sure you don't run audio / video wiring parallel to power cables for more than 2m – this can negatively affect picture and sound quality. Keep them 0.5m apart and, if they have to cross, make sure it's at 90 degrees.

EQUIPMENT

■ Tape measure
■ Drill
■ Spirit level
■ Pencil
For stud wall
■ Stud finder
■ Hammer
■ Thin nail

How to...
wall-mount an HDTV

1 Preparation

If your wall is made of solid brick or breeze blocks, you have a reasonably simple job and can go to Step 2. If it's an internal stud wall, you'll need a stud finder (around £15 from *www.amazon.co.uk*) to locate the wooden studs. You can't simply drill into the plasterboard at random; plasterboard alone won't be able to take the weight, but the wooden studs will. Once you've found the studs, hammer a thin nail through the plasterboard to verify the stud is there, then move it 10mm to the left and repeat until you find empty space. Do the same to the right and then mark where the centre line of the stud is (studs usually run vertically).

2 Drill the holes

On the rear of the TV, you may need to use a screwdriver to remove the stand and any blanking plates covering the mounting holes, and then attach the mounting bracket. Measure the distance between the bottom of the TV to the lowermost screw holes on the part of the bracket that attaches to the wall. Then, mark the wall where you want the bottom of the TV to be and use the earlier measurement to work out where to drill the holes – use a spirit level to keep it straight. Make sure the screws you're using are appropriate for the weight of your HDTV and, if drilling into masonry, make sure the Rawlplugs are similarly heavy-duty.

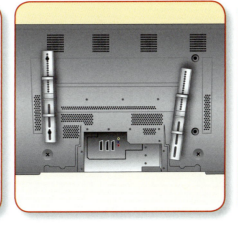

3 The bracket

Once you've attached the other part of the bracket to the wall, enlist the help of another person to lift the TV into place while you attach it to the bracket. If you have an adjustable bracket, again use the spirit level to make sure it's level and, for tilt-and-swivel brackets, work it through the whole range to make sure everything is working solidly. Tilting brackets are particularly useful if you have to mount the HDTV higher than you would have liked, since they make viewing more comfortable and can help avoid reflections.

4 Cabling

Now you can attach your cabling. Once the TV is in place, connect the power, audio and video cables. When you're buying these cables, make sure you've carefully measured the distance they'll need to cover and then add around 15% to make sure there's enough slack. Test each one and make sure everything is connecting as it should, working them into whatever cable-management system you've settled on. Then, you can simply sit back and enjoy some high-definition action. Well done...

53

HD switches

The number of HD sources is growing faster than the number of inputs on your TV. So what happens when you run out of sockets?

Unless you've just bought a top-of-the-line HDTV, chances are that it won't have much more than two HDMI sockets and one component input. If you've got a model more than a year old, it may have just one of each.

That may not seem much of a problem at the moment, but you could soon find it becoming a limiting factor. After all, if you've invested in a high-definition TV, it makes sense to feed it with as many HD sources as possible.

So what to do once you've added that brand-new Blu-ray player, Sky HD and an Xbox 360 to your setup? Thankfully, there's an easy answer in the form of switch boxes. They may not be glamorous, but they'll allow you to plug numerous sources into a single input, and switch between them at will.

Go your own way

At the most basic, if you just want to expand the number of HDMI ports you have to play with, there are plenty of options on the market. To split an input two ways, for example, you can spend as little as £10, although you'll get what you pay for. You should also check whether splitters will support the latest HDMI v1.3b standard – cheaper models often won't. If you've more inputs to contend with (or you're just planning for the future), take a look at Lindy's HDMI 1.3b Switch Remote. It will combine four sources and comes with

a remote control for selecting the input. Factor in that you'll need to buy new cables too, though, and you may as well buy a better TV with more inputs. Better value is Belkin's PureAV HDMI Interface 3-to-1 Video Switch, which will cope with three inputs, and at less than half the price.

For when you have multiple component video inputs to contend with (such as those from an upscaling DVD player), Joytech has a switch box to match – the Control Center 540C combines five inputs of Xbox 360, HD component video or composite video along with analogue or digital audio for just £20. For the more ambitious, there's Joytech's AV Control Center 245C, which can handle up to seven inputs in the same format as the 540C – without the Xbox 360 input – for a mere £45.

The old way

If you're happy to swap round cables manually, but want to protect the input port on the back of your TV, the Lindy HDMI Port Saver will prevent it working loose prematurely. Costing a paltry £9, it will also make recessed ports easier to access when switching. You can also get angled versions for awkwardly placed sockets.

Finally, if you still have multiple standard-definition sources to deal with as well, the £10 Multi-Scart Switching Unit from Maplin will allow you to use three devices on the same input and switch between them manually. 🔄

HDMI

HDMI sockets are the only connections you should ideally be using when viewing HD content. Not only do they offer the best quality, but they also carry digital audio at the same time. So make sure you have enough for the future.

➲ **Lindy 4 PortHDMI 1.3 Switch Remote**	
Price	£105
Internet	www.lindy.com/uk
Rating	★★★☆☆

➲ **Maplin Multi-Scart Switching Unit**	
Price	£10
Internet	www.maplin.co.uk
Rating	★★★☆☆

➲ **Joytech Control Center 540C**	
Price	£20
Internet	www.joytechstore.net
Rating	★★★★☆

➲ **Lindy 2 Port HDMI Switch**	
Price	£55
Internet	www.lindy.com/uk
Rating	★★★☆☆

➲ **Joytech AV Control Center 245C**	
Price	£45
Internet	www.joytechstore.net
Rating	★★★☆☆

➲ **Belkin PureAV HDMI Interface 3-to-1 Video Switch**	
Price	£45
Internet	http://catalog.belkin.com
Rating	★★★★☆

Fine-tune your picture (basic)

Get the most out of your TV – old or new – by taking the time to properly adjust the basic brightness and contrast settings

High contrast:
A better contrast ratio makes for a more impressive picture.

Low contrast:
Don't make do with this washed-out feel.

There are those who'll fork out a fortune for a new TV, plonk it in their living room, power it up and sink happily into the sofa. While there's nothing wrong with that, we'll let you into a secret – their TV will look rubbish.

The fact is that TVs aren't set up to look perfect out of the box, and some are even deliberately made to look as garish and unnatural as possible so they stand out in the shop. Unlike the good old days of three knobs sat on the front of the set, modern TV menus contain a daunting number of options, covering all sorts of adjustments. Thankfully, though, you only really need to touch a couple of these to make 95% of the difference.

The first of these is colour temperature. Don't worry about what it does for now, but the main reason for its existence is so that it can be tweaked in the showroom to boost warmth, which is sadly at the cost of accuracy. So if you have this setting in your menu, the first step is to set this at 6300K (this setting might also simply be called 'neutral') to give a level playing field and view colours at their most natural.

After that, the most important controls are also the most commonly known: brightness (which is actually black level) and contrast (white level). Setting these is vital to get a proper picture from your TV: they define the contrast ratio you're seeing – the difference between the blackest black and the whitest white. We've all seen washed-out pictures

or those that lose detail in the lightest or darkest areas of an image; these problems can usually be simply fixed by setting brightness and contrast properly.

The best way to calibrate your picture is to display a 'control' image that contains the whitest white and the blackest black, and use it to manually adjust the settings. You may already have such an image without knowing it: any THX-Certified DVD – most Pixar movies, for example – contains a THX Optimizer application, which has all the tests necessary to set up your picture in the home.

You'll want to let the TV warm up for ten minutes first, and run the tests in the same lighting conditions you'd normally watch your favourite movies or shows in, as the ambient light will affect the results. Adjusting in a brightly lit room will result in a brighter picture than a lamp-lit room in the evening, and bear in mind that the films themselves are usually mastered in a moderately dark room.

The process itself involves gradually tweaking both the brightness and contrast levels to achieve the optimum balance, as shown in the walkthrough on the right, and it's worth repeating the basic routine every few months as your TV ages. Then, while you can easily leave it there and just get on with watching your favourite movies in glorious HD, don't forget the myriad other adjustments that can make your picture even more accurate. It's these we'll be looking at over the page. ⒤

How to...
use the THX Optimizer

While it's possible to have your TV professionally calibrated, it's much more convenient – not to mention cheaper – to do it yourself

1 Start the THX Optimizer

Once you've allowed your TV to warm up and switched your lighting to closely resemble your film-viewing atmosphere, you'll be ready to load up the THX Optimizer application. Its location within the menu will differ from DVD to DVD – in this example, *Terminator 2: Ultimate Edition*, it's rather well hidden in the Sensory Control (video and audio) menu, on the bolt on the cyborg's head. Choose Video Tests to begin: the exact tests may vary depending on the age of your DVD, but each will be prefaced by an instruction screen.

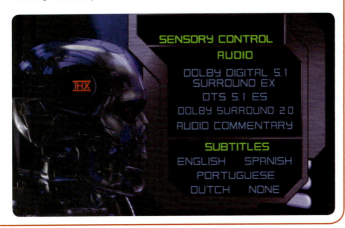

2 Adjust the contrast

The eight boxes contain one of four different shades of white, all placed on a totally black background. Begin with your TV's contrast up high – the boxes will all look washed out, don't worry – then gradually reduce it until the large white area is bright but low enough that you can clearly distinguish all four different shades from each other. At this point, the brightest of the whites will then represent the highest white you'll see in that particular film, although this will be much the same in any modern film.

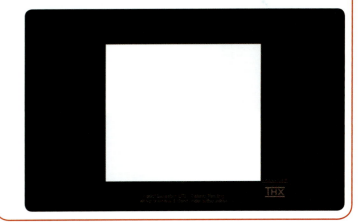

3 Adjust the brightness

With the contrast now set, the next test screen displays a series of greyscale blocks on a black background, along with a THX logo in faint grey. Start with the brightness up high, then gradually lower it until you can just about make out the THX letters, but not see the drop shadow behind the lettering. An alternative method is to use the black boxes along the top: adjust your brightness down until the seventh darkest box disappears, then turn it back up slowly until you can just make out that seventh box. This should give you the optimum brightness setting.

4 Check the results

At this point, you can skip the remaining tests and go straight to the final test – a short clip from the feature on the DVD, chosen for its blend of colours and lighting. Look at the areas of shadow – are they too murky and dark? Look at the light colours – do they appear washed out? If the picture doesn't look right, go back to the beginning of the THX Optimizer and start again, and if you still can't tweak it to your satisfaction you may need to turn the page and use some of the more advanced settings to get the picture the way you want it.

Fine-tune your picture (advanced)

Once you've set the brightness and contrast, there are plenty of other ways to make sure you're getting the best possible picture

Fine-tuning colour: You'll often find TVs set up at their most vibrant settings by default...

...but a little adjustment will yield far more natural results.

Once you've set up the basic brightness and contrast levels to your satisfaction, you're most of the way to getting the best picture out of your TV. But there's still plenty more tinkering you could do: you might be left with colours that seem a little off, fuzzy edges or even something as jarring as a squashed image on the screen. At this stage, it's time to delve in the 'advanced settings' menu.

The array of adjustments available varies between sets, but many will at least allow you to tweak the basic colour settings from the defaults. As mentioned on the previous page, the THX Optimizer application on any THX-Certified DVD has a test to help you accurately set the colour (or saturation) and tint (or hue) of your display. Like the brightness and contrast tests, this application works by displaying a specially designed test pattern that mimics the colour section of the SMPTE test card – the standard set of colour bars used by video studios worldwide.

If you have the THX blue-tinted glasses (available from *www.thx.com*), you can use the special blue test image. But on the reasonable assumption that you didn't think to buy them when you bought that copy of *Toy Story 2*, you can just as easily use the colour bar section of the Monitor Performance pattern as a naked-eye substitute.

Sharpness is an interesting setting, far less important for HDTV broadcasts than it is for standard ones. The reason is that an SD broadcast on an HDTV needs that little bit of fuzziness to mask the lack of resolution; by contrast, an HD broadcast can benefit greatly from a bit of sharpening as it has the necessary definition to display the sharp edges that result. Too much sharpness, however, can make the picture appear noisy, so use sparingly, and do an A:B comparison between HD and SD sources.

And finally, don't forget the basics – it's amazing how often they're missed. The Monitor Check and Aspect Ratio Setup sections of the THX Optimizer application display some geometric shapes to help ensure you have the picture correctly positioned and orientated, and that there's no panoramic zooming or aspect-ratio fudging being 'helpfully' applied by an overzealous TV.

Once you've done everything else, you can run the final test – a selected scene from the movie you're using as the test DVD. Chosen for its use of colour and detail, you should be able to get a good idea of how well you've done. If it doesn't look right, go back and try the necessary steps again until it does. It'll be worth it in the end... Ⓖ

How to...
tweak tint and sharpness

The rest of the THX Optimizer deals with colour and sharpness. Once you've dealt with brightness and contrast, spend a further five minutes on these

1 Colour and tint

If you've ordered the THX Optimizer blue-tinted glasses, you can make use of the proper colour and tint test image. Although it appears to be made up of cyan, magenta, blue and white boxes, when viewed through the glasses it should look like solid blue bars if your TV is set up correctly. If not, adjust the hue and saturation gradually in your TV's menu until you can eliminate the individual colours completely. Even if your TV won't let you adjust colour/saturation and tint/hue, this test will at least tell you whether it's displaying the proper values.

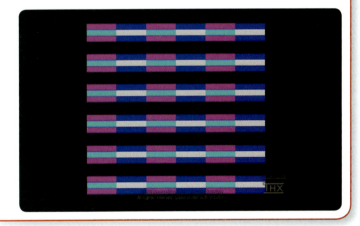

2 With the naked eye

If you don't have the Optimizer glasses, you could also skip straight to the next test – called Monitor Performance – for a more subjective colour test. It's designed for adjusting other settings, but the colour bar towards the top can be used for colour and tint: first, adjust your colour/saturation control until the red box is red but not bleeding (that is, the red isn't spilling over into the neighbouring colour), then adjust the hue/tint until the cyan and magenta boxes appear truly cyan and magenta in colour, without being overblown.

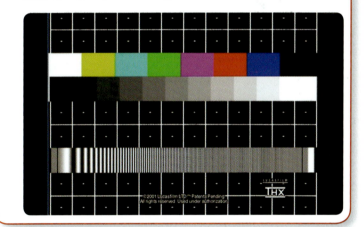

3 Sharpness

The same test image can be used to adjust sharpness, which is particularly useful for HD images. Looking at the band of vertical black and white bars across the lower half of the screen, raise the sharpness until the lines become 'edgy', then reduce it again until the lines are well-defined, but not overly enhanced. If you apply too much sharpness – over-enhancing – the picture can appear too crisp and noisy, while the opposite can make an image appear slightly out of focus. This may be beneficial with SD video, but for HD it will greatly reduce the impact.

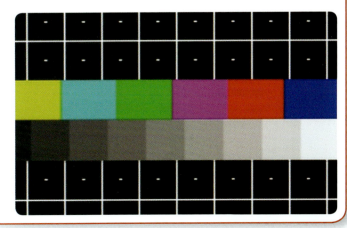

4 Geometry

The remaining tests are to determine whether your TV and DVD player are set to the correct aspect ratio. They consist of two screens – one for 4:3 displays, the other for 16:9 – with a circle in a box. If correctly displayed, the box should stretch all around the outer edge of the screen and the circle should be round. If there are black bars above and below the box, your DVD player is probably set to output 4:3; if the image is squashed horizontally, your monitor is probably set to 4:3. When satisfied, run the final test video to see the fruits of your labour.

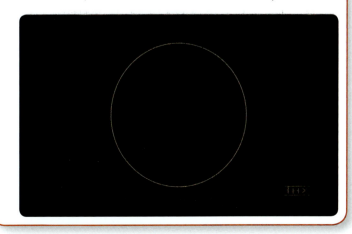

59

Boosting your Freeview signal

A weak digital signal can lead to stuttering pictures or even prevent you receiving channels. We explain the potential causes

By far the easiest and cheapest way to receive digital TV is via Freeview. All you need is an inexpensive set-top box – or a digital tuner in your TV – and a decent signal from your television aerial. Unfortunately, only three-quarters of UK households can currently receive Freeview (*see p16*), and even those can sometimes struggle to get an adequate signal. But before you resign yourself to getting a satellite dish or cable (*see p66*), follow our guide to boosting your Freeview signal.

Signal failure

The first thing to do is enter your postcode into the signal checker at *www.freeview.co.uk/availability*. If you're not in a Freeview area, you're simply wasting money by investing in new aerials or signal boosters, but at least you know that satellite, cable or internet services are your best bet.

In a Freeview area but can't receive any channels? Delve into your set-top box's menu settings and make sure it's set to automatically scan for new channels. This is important if you've just moved house, as the Freeview channel transmissions differ from area to area, and you should perform a new manual search in the new area.

If you can only receive certain channels or overall reception is prone to interference or stuttering, then there's a plethora of potential causes. Start by switching to one of the channels you're having trouble with, enter the Freeview box's menu system and look for a Signal Strength option. If this is weak, the problem may well lie with your television aerial, many of which are decades old.

Freeview usually works best with an external 'wideband' aerial. If you're using an indoor antenna or an aerial in the roof space of your house, you may need to invest in an external aerial – seek advice from a trained expert from the Confederation of Aerial Industries (*www.cai.org.uk*).

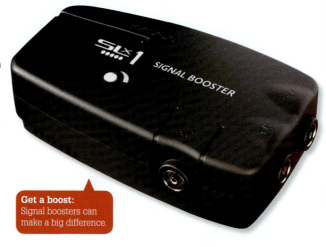

Get a boost:
Signal boosters can make a big difference.

Signal strength:
Hi-gain aerials can improve Freeview's signal stength.

A social problem

People living in flats with a communal aerial can often suffer from patchy reception, since the signal is shared between a number of properties. A signal booster may help, especially if it's only one or two channels that you're struggling with – just make sure you get it as close to the aerial as you can. If the signal's particularly weak, an amplified indoor aerial might be a better option, especially if you're on a high floor. Alternatively, ask your landlord or freeholder to consider investing in an Integrated Reception System (IRS) to distribute the signal more effectively between multiple users.

Believe it or not, you can also suffer from too much signal. If you're living close to a transmitter, the signal strength can overpower your Freeview box, which can lead to interference. If your box is showing near-perfect signal levels, try buying an aerial attenuator from your local electrical shop to see if that makes a difference.

Keeping it clean

Other possible causes of interference include poor cabling and other electrical appliances in the house. Check that cables aren't fraying or damaged, replacing where necessary; avoid signal splitters and extension leads where possible, and consider using signal boosters if you're struggling to get a picture on secondary sets in bedrooms or kitchens. Running the TV aerial through VCRs or DVD players can also significantly weaken the signal – try plugging the aerial lead directly into the Freeview box to see if it makes a difference.

Finally, microwaves, boilers and mobile phones can also interfere with digital television signals – keep your Freeview box as far away from these devices as possible to achieve interference-free viewing. ⓘ

Configuring sound

A modern TV should offer plenty of control over audio settings, from treble and bass to the mysteriously named SRS. Here, we explain how to take full advantage

SETTING UP

INTRO | CHOOSING | BUYING | SETTING UP | ENJOYING HD | HD ON YOUR PC | EXPANSION | HD HOME

A s with the picture quality, you may have to do some tweaking to achieve the best sound from your TV. Thankfully, most sets make this reasonably simple.

The integrated speakers in most TVs are easy to set up, as they don't have many controls. And don't worry if your HDTV doesn't have all the features we mention here, as some of the controls are available only on more expensive sets.

It's important to get it right, though, particularly when it comes to treble and bass. There are no hard and fast rules, but finding the right balance will ensure you'll hear dialogue and get the impact of sound effects. Find a scene from a film with plenty of loud noises and explosions and set your volume to normal listening levels. Start with the bass at its lowest setting and adjust it upwards until you have a rich, deep-sounding bass. You know you've gone too far when the bass drowns out everything else, you have distortion or everything sounds 'muddy'. For treble, pick a scene with music or dialogue and start from the top down. You're aiming to pick out the higher frequencies clearly without making the sound too shrill or tinny.

Most televisions also have an option for SRS – a way of generating fake surround sound using just stereo speakers. When you turn it on, you may find that sound suddenly becomes very quiet depending on what you're watching. It's a mixed blessing: SRS usually works well on films and busy soundtracks, but for documentaries with just a single voice-over

it doesn't always do a good job. So you may have to use SRS when it sounds good, and turn it off when it doesn't.

If your TV has the option for volume levelling, you can use it to reduce the effect of adverts being too loud. Levelling lets you set a maximum volume for the TV, automatically reducing loud noises. It's also useful for watching films at night, as you can prevent explosions and the like from waking the rest of the household – but it will limit the impact.

Outside help

If you've added external speakers, the best way to give them the once-over is to get hold of a THX-certified DVD (*see p58*). Visit *www.thx.com* to get a list of the current movies that feature the test utility. As with its picture setup routine, it will walk you through each stage, allowing you to adjust each speaker so it has the same volume from wherever you're watching from.

Finally, the tests help you to find out if any of your speakers are out of phase. When a speaker is out of phase, its driver moves out while the other speakers' drivers move in. The result is that you get imprecise sound that can ruin the carefully crafted soundtrack. This can be fixed by ensuring that all speakers are wired up correctly. Again, check the THX website for full information on the tests, but follow the instructions on a suitable disc to ensure the highest-quality audio – and never be afraid to listen to what your ears are telling you. ⊕

Aspect ratios

Get the best quality out of your HDTV by ensuring your video sources – and the TV – are set up with the right aspect ratio

The ideal situation: 16:9 video showing on a 16:9 screen, just as nature intended.

Stretching 4:3 content to fit a 16:9 screen is a common mistake – it may make the most of your screen size, but it distorts the picture horribly.

TIP

If the extreme left and right edges of the image seem to be stretched but the rest of the picture is normal, your HDTV may have a non-linear panorama mode. This is the theoretically happy compromise between black bars at the top and bottom of the screen and stretching the whole image to fit. However, some HDTVs handle this better than others, and the effect may be too distracting to watch. If so, find the 'zoom' option in the menu and switch it to 1:1.

Aspect ratios are perhaps the least understood issue in the home cinema world, HDTVs included. It's a classic mistake in home and shops alike – if you're watching a TV show or film and people look too fat or too thin, chances are the aspect ratio is wrongly set – even if the picture is filling the whole screen.

The principles of aspect ratios are easy to understand – it's the width of the video in relation to the height. For example, HDTVs have an aspect ratio of 16:9, so they're 78% wider than they are tall. By contrast, older TVs had a 4:3 ratio, leaving them only 33% wider than they were tall. A 16:9 TV is a more natural aspect ratio, since this aspect ratio is closer to your field of vision.

Not all widescreen video has a 16:9 aspect ratio, though – films transferred from cinefilm, for example, may be even wider at 2.35:1 or 1.85:1. In this instance, the disc, player or HDTV might leave black bars at the top and bottom, it may stretch the video to fit or zoom in, cutting off the left- and right-hand edges. And each may do something different.

It's important to know what your HDTV (as well as your DVD player or set-top box) is doing with the video it's receiving or sending, as you could be watching degraded quality. Most video sources and HDTVs have aspect ratio or zoom controls, so look in the menus to check they're all set to 16:9, which should also keep any 4:3 aspect TV channels in check, and beware of any 'smart' options.

Some HDTVs won't give you aspect ratio control when the incoming video is 720p, 1080i or 1080p, only allowing you to control them when standard-definition videos are being shown. This means you may get black bars at the top and bottom (or left and right on 4:3 broadcasts), although purists would argue this is only right, and that footage should be viewed as originally intended anyway.

Native resolution

Having an HDTV that doesn't change the aspect ratio of the incoming signal can actually be a benefit. If you're playing a 1080p Blu-ray disc, and you've connected the player to your 1080p HDTV using an HDMI cable, you don't want the digital signal to be altered in any way.

Assuming your TV has an actual 1080 pixel height, each pixel of every frame of the video is directly 'mapped' to the same pixel of your HDTV, and not upscaled or downscaled in any way. This leads to the best possible image quality, with objects naturally having the correct proportions.

With your HDTV in this mode, it may simply display all incoming video formats as they are, regardless of their resolution. This could leave black bars on all sides, not just the top and bottom. For example, a 720p video displayed natively on a 1080p HDTV would be a 1280 x 720 window within the 1920 x 1080 display. Fortunately, most HDTVs are intelligent enough to upscale 720p video while leaving 1080p and 1080i sources alone. The only downside is that you may see interference or a solid white line along the top or bottom edge of the screen.

A native mode on a 720p HDTV is potentially the most useful scenario, since the actual resolution of most panels is 1366 x 768. If a 720p video were to fill the entire screen, it would have to be upscaled, which inevitably degrades quality. But if the HDTV leaves the incoming signal alone, it will display each of the 720 video lines on a line of pixels, leaving small black borders. Although the image will be smaller, it will be sharper and the quality will appear better. If this is something you'd like to have control over, it's worth making sure any HD equipment you buy includes some form of aspect ratio control – which generally involves going for mid-range or premium end models. *iG*

"You may get black bars at the top and bottom, although purists would argue this is only right..."

Anamorphic video

Traditional anamorphic video is a technique where the camera's lens squeezes a wide image horizontally, so that it fits in a standard 1.33:1 aspect ratio. Although this will rarely affect owners of modern HDTVs, there are still devices that use anamorphic video, including DVD players.

Many HD camcorders use the technique, primarily to save on the cost of having a full HD (1920 x 1080) sensor. They use a 1440 x 1080 sensor but change the aspect ratio of individual pixels, so each pixel isn't 1:1 but is in fact 1.33:1. If you could actually see an individual anamorphic frame pixel for pixel, circles would appear like tall ellipses. But, because of the 1.33:1 pixels, when this video is played back on your HDTV the ellipse becomes a perfect circle again. All you need to do is make sure your DVD player and TV are both set to 16:9.

Anamorphic video uses a 1.33:1 pixel ratio to squeeze widescreen images into 4:3 recordings.

16:9 ratio
4:3 ratio

CHAPTER **5** | **Enjoying HD**

Now you're ready to sit back and reap the rewards of all your hard work. There are plenty of places to find great high-definition content these days, from satellite and cable operators to a shiny new generation of video discs battling it out for supremacy, plus the very latest in games consoles. All isn't lost for your old DVDs and home movies, either, as we unravel how to make the best of standard-definition content on your HD screen. And if you're wondering how long it will be until we're all watching the good old Beeb in HD, we'll uncover the UK's HD future.

HDT.V services

Increasing the number of channels will help you get the most out of your equipment. Here, we look at the available HD options

Freeview is a huge improvement over the old analogue system, and the range of channels you can get for no cost is rather impressive. But it isn't in high definition – or, at least, it isn't yet. And it isn't the only free option, either. So if you want the best possible pictures (not to mention an even wider choice of movies, sports and entertainment) you'll need to turn to Freeview's satellite cousin, Freesat, or be willing to pay for a subscription-based service such as Sky HD or Virgin Media XL. Both offer a competitive range of packages, starting with entry-level options that contain just a few channels, all the way up to the top-level packages, which include movies and sports.

Freesat
Launched in 2008 as a competitor to Freeview, Freesat is a joint venture between the BBC and ITV. It works in much the same way as its terrestrial forebear except that, instead of an aerial, you need a satellite in order to receive the Freesat channels. If you've already got an Astra-compatible dish installed (such as an old Sky one), you then just need a set-top box to receive the 200+ channels – only two of which of which are currently in HD, including. Fitting a dish will cost you around £80 (see *www.freesat.co.uk* for guidance on that), and an HD set-top box a further £120 (cheaper ones will be SD-capable only). Freesat boxes with built-in PVRs are on the horizon too.

Sky HD
Sky has the most popular digital television service, but to get it you'll need to have a satellite dish installed. This is possible for the vast majority of people, although you may need permission or a special installation. To get HD channels, you'll also need a Sky HD set-top box, which currently costs £299, plus a one-off fee of £30. There's also a monthly £10 fee on top of any subscription you've got.

In use, the Sky HD box is the same as Sky+, with two tuners so you can record two channels at the same time. It's also got a 320GB hard disk inside, although only 160GB is available for recordings (the rest used for a rotating library of content). This equates to around 80 hours of recordings. The set-top box has proved to be reliable, and it's both well designed and easy to use. Sky's electronic programming guide (EPG) is fairly quick to update and lets you set your recordings quickly at the touch of a button.

Virgin Media
Virgin Media is Sky's main competitor and was formed after the Virgin parent company bought the merged Telewest and NTL cable providers. It offers a similar range of channels to Sky, although there's no Sky One, due to a well-publicised falling out between the companies over pricing in 2007.

Unlike Sky, Virgin Media's service is delivered over high-speed, fibre-optic cabling in the ground. While this means you only need a single cable to put in your house for

	BT Vision	Sky HD	Virgin Media XL
Price	£199 + £30 installation fee	£299 + £30 fee/£10 a month + normal subscription	£150 installation fee/ £25 a month
HD programming	✗	✓	✓
HD channels	0	20	1
Supported HD formats	720p, 1080i	720p, 1080i	720p, 1080i
On-demand	Library of films, TV and music, some HD	80 hours of Sky Anytime	Library of films, TV and music, some HD
TV tuners	2 (Freeview)	2	3
Hard disk	160GB	320GB (160GB reserved for Sky Anytime)	160GB
Hours of recording	80	80	80
Outputs	Scart and HDMI	Scart, component and HDMI	Scart, component and HDMI
Requirements	BT Total Broadband	Satellite dish	Availability of cable sevice

SKY
Sky started transmitting HD content in May 2006. The service currently has twenty subscription channels including sports, plus two pay-per-view movie channels. It costs £10 on top of an existing Sky subscription, plus a one-off cost for the HD set-top box.

FIVE
Five hasn't announced a firm HD launch to date. However, with the rights to top US programming, such as *Prison Break* and *Supernatural*, that's available in HD, we're waiting with baited breath.

VIRGIN MEDIA
You can view HD content here, too, working on a pay-per-view basis. You can also receive BBC HD. Packages vary, but the initial cost is usually £150 for the set-top box.

CHANNEL 4
Channel 4 HD is currently only to Sky HD subscribers. However, the company has previously shown interest in broadcasting on the Freesat service too, so it may not remain so forever.

ITV
ITV HD is currently an exclusively Freesat offering, and kicked off with UEFA 2008. No word on how long it'll be before we see it on other platforms.

BBC
The BBC HD channel is available on Vigin Media, Sky HD and Freesat. After running as a trial, it became permanent in Dec 2007. It runs for a few hours a day, often simulcasting with other BBC channels.

> ## "With BT Vision, you can pay £4 a month to watch every Premiership match after it's been played"

a range of services, you also have to live in a cable area. This excludes many small villages and private roads, who have no choice but to go down the Sky route.

To get HD, you'll also need a V+ set-top box. There's a one-off installation fee of £150 and a monthly £5 fee for the M and L TV packages; subscribers to XL don't have to pay this. Technically speaking, V+ is more advanced than Sky+, as it has three tuners so you can record two channels while watching a third. The box has a 160GB hard disk, all of which is available for recordings, so giving you around 80 hours of storage. As the set-top box is rented from Virgin Media, any technical problems will be fixed or the box replaced. Virgin Media's EPG is similar to Sky's, although we've found it a touch more sluggish.

HD channels
Choosing a service is likely to depend on what you want to watch. If it's live TV in HD, then Sky has by far the best choice. Depending on your subscription, there's a choice of ten HD channels, including Sky Sports, Sky One, BBC HD and the Discovery Channel. Currently, it's the only way to watch Premiership football in HD.

Virgin Media has just BBC HD available as a live, high-definition channel, which sounds quite poor. However, there's an excellent on-demand service that goes a long way towards making up for it. This service plays your choice of programme live from Virgin Media's servers over the cable network. As you don't need to download or store any of these programmes, the library of choice is as big as Virgin Media wants it to be, and it's growing every day. Here, you'll find a wide choice of films with prices from £2 to £3.50 (£4.50 for high-definition films) including every

single Bond film from *Dr No* to *Casino Royale*. Each 'rental' is available to watch for 24 hours, so you have the pleasure and flexibility of choosing what you want to watch when you want to watch it.

If you choose the XL package, there's even better news, as you get TV Choice on demand for free, so you can watch complete series of shows such as *Lost*, *Curb Your Enthusiasm* and *Band of Brothers*. Again, the interface is a little sluggish, but the choice is staggering.

This is light years ahead of what Sky can offer. As Sky uses satellites, it can only broadcast to all of its subscribers at once. Its answer is to use 160GB of your 320GB Sky HD box to store a series of programmes and films that you can then access instantly. With 80 hours of programming, there's a good chance you'll find something to fit the mood, but the list is always changing to make way for new content, and you simply can't access anything that isn't already stored there.

Broadband TV
If it's on-demand that you want then BT Vision could be the answer. You'll need a BT Total Broadband account to receive the service, which includes a BT V-box set-top box. This contains two Freeview tuners and a 160GB hard disk (again, good for around 80 hours of recordings) so you can do a similar range of things to both the Sky+ and V+ boxes. It's the on-demand services that are of more interest, though, as you can stream a similar range of content to Virgin Media's service live from BT's servers.

These include complete series' (from 29p per episode), movies (from £1.99 a film) and music videos. You can also pay £4 a month to watch every Premiership match after it's been played, stump up for Setanta Sports (£11 a month) or do both. There's an HDMI output on the back, as well as a reasonable selection of HD content, first introduced in 2008. Unlike a true on-demand service though, it needs to be downloaded to your V-Box before you can watch it. This should hopefully change as broadband speeds increase.

67

⮂ BT VISION

Price	£199 + £30
Internet	www.btvision.bt.com
Rating	★★★☆☆

BT Vision requires you to switch to BT Total Broadband: a big put-off if you're happy with your current ISP. You get a V-box Freeview PVR with twin tuners and 160GB of disk space for 80 hours of recording. As with Virgin Media V+ and Sky HD, you can record entire series' at the click of a button.

BT Vision's real strength is its selection of on-demand programming. The films aren't always cutting edge and you pay for each TV episode you watch, so it isn't as good value for heavy consumers, but sports are available through Setanta Sports (£11 a month), and you can watch every Premiership game after it's been played for £4 a month. A decent wadge of HD content is now available, although it has to be downloaded in full before you can watch it, which isn't anywhere near as satisfying as an instant hit.

⮂ SKY HD

Price	£75 + £30 installation fee/ £10 a month + normal subscription
Internet	www.sky.com
Rating	★★★★☆

If you want the best choice of HD channels (and particularly football), Sky is the obvious option. The box is reasonably priced (if not the a £10 monthly fee for HD), and you do get a reliable service and a great choice. Sky's EPG makes it easy to select what you want to record, and 80 hours of footage available on the 320GB disk should be enough for all but the busiest TV fan.

On-demand services are limited to the other 80 hours that Sky broadcasts to the reserved disk space on your box. These are refreshed often, so there's no back catalogue of older TV or movies to watch. But until Sky ties its box into broadband or cable, that's as on-demand as it will get. That said, if you're more interested in live TV than picking from a wide range of older shows, Sky HD remains the best option.

⮂ VIRGIN MEDIA XL

Price	£150 installation fee / £25 a month
Internet	www.virginmedia.com
Rating	★★★★★

Virgin Media's excellent three-tuner V+ box comes with every TV package, but it's with the XL package that you'll really get your money's worth. Subscribe to this and you get TV Choice on demand, which gives you access to lots of complete series of TV shows for free. It's like having a massive DVD library, and the list of shows is growing all of the time. There's a wide range of movies to pick from, too, including old classics and the latest blockbusters. Some (but definitely not all) of this content is in HD, too.

Only BBC HD is available as a live high-definition channel. You can subscribe to Sky Sports (if only the standard-definition channels), although you do get Setanta Sports for free. There's no Sky One, but if American series and HD sports aren't that important, then Virgin Media's service is better value than Sky's – and its on-demand programming is amazing.

FREESAT

From £40 (SD) / £120 (HD)
www.freesat.co.uk
★★★★☆

Like its terrestrial cousin Freeview, Freesat has no subscription, so it's up to third parties to provide the decoding hardware. While you can get TVs with Freesat built in (*see p42*), you'll currently have a much broader choice getting a set-top box (*see right*). If you've already got an Astra-compatible satellite dish installed (such as a Sky one), you can just pop one of these boxes onto it and get over 130 free channels. If not, it'll cost you £80 (building regulations and tenancy agreements permitting) to get one fitted.

Only BBC HD and ITV HD are available as yet, but it's certainly the best lineup, and unlike the Freeview option, there's little to stop more being added – in fact, dozens are possible. PVR, or Freesat+ recording boxes came onto the market in November 2008 – check out *www.igizmo.co.uk* for the latest recommendations.

The future of HDTV in the UK

Free-to-air HD broadcasting in the UK has been slow to appear but it is happening – we reveal what's next

HD movies and games consoles may be ideal for showing off those big new screens, but it's good old broadcast television that still takes up most of our time on the sofa. Although 3.8 million of us have invested hundreds or thousands of pounds in HDTVs, the vast majority still only receive TV programmes in standard PAL at a piffling resolution of 720 x 576. And even those who've signed up to HD subscription services such as Sky HD (see left) still receive much of their TV in this format. So how long before we can all get free-to-air HD broadcasts in our homes?

High production values

Naturally, to broadcast a TV programme in HD, it has to be shot in HD (or film). Thankfully, the TV industry has been quick to move over to the new technology. In the US, HD production has been going on for years and these days all major TV dramas (think *Lost* and *Heroes*) are shot in HD. The BBC, on the other hand, shot its first HD drama, *Bleak House*, in early 2005; quickly followed by *Planet Earth* (see p76) and live sporting events, including Wimbledon. The BBC has stated that it wants to be producing all its content in HD by 2010, but we're still some years away from there being a big enough library of HD content to fill the number of channels we currently enjoy through Freeview. So no repeats of *The Good Life* in HD, then.

Constricting waves

As bleak as it may sound, there aren't likely to be very many terrestrially broadcast HD channels in the near future. This is due to them taking up around five times the bandwidth of a standard-definition stream. This space is limited by the available UHF frequencies, pretty much all of which are taken up by the current system – there simply isn't enough space to broadcast a range of HD channels to the aerial on your roof (hence why Freesat was born).

However, the old analogue TV signal takes up around half of the frequencies between 200MHz and 1GHz. These are the best available frequencies thanks to a combination of good bandwidth and decent range, giving the coverage needed. As the analogue signal is turned off between 2008 and 2012 (see p16), those frequencies could become available for HD broadcasts.

Digital dividend

However, this isn't as straightforward as either we or broadcasters such as the BBC and Channel 4 wish. Just because the frequencies are being freed up by turning off TV stations, there's no guarantee that they'll be gifted back to the broadcasters to replace HD channels. A number of other options are being considered, including wireless broadband networks and mobile phone services. The BBC and others have put forward a proposal that gives them

enough space for five terrestrial HD channels, enough (they say) to satisfy the viewer.

The BBC itself has been running a trial HD channel since May 2006. This shows around five hours of HD programming a day and is available to subscribers of Sky's and Virgin Media's HD services. It's also available via free-to-air satellite and, for a limited time, was broadcast to a small trial area in London via terrestrial DVB-T broadcast known as Freeview HD. The satellite broadcast is unscrambled and can be received by anyone with the correct equipment. But you'll need a satellite dish, and either a special set-top box or a powerful PC with a satellite or terrestrial TV tuner.

The trial has been a success, though, and the BBC is now planning a single, permanent HD channel to be broadcast on cable and satellite services for around nine hours a day, showing BBC1 and BBC2 programmes in HD. A terrestrial broadcast channel may also be available, but would be limited to only four hours overnight due to a lack of available bandwidth. Those with HD-capable set-top boxes could then record these broadcasts and watch the programmes the following evening.

Cabling up

For the time being then, it's satellite and cable TV providers who'll provide the vast majority of HD broadcasts, and you'll have to pay if you want to receive them. Opposite, we've detailed the two competing services available from Sky and Virgin Media.

To really get the HD bandwagon rolling, though, these providers will need free-to-air broadcasters, like the BBC, ITV, Channel 4 and Five, to expand or launch their own HD services. ITV HD is currently a Freesat exclusive, although it will start appearing on other platforms before long. Channel 4, meanwhile, has 4HD, which you can only find (for now) on Sky HD. It's a simulcast of 'the core Channel 4 schedule', so you can expect a good deal of it (with US dramas and recent C4 productions) to be in HD.

Net cast

A final option is to abandon the airwaves, satellites and traditional cable TV systems and get HDTV from your internet connection. It's already possible (although illegal) to use file-sharing sites to download many of the latest episodes of US dramas in HD, and its popularity shows there is the demand. However, legal services are starting to appear. Sadly, while we had high hopes for the Xbox 360 Live Video store, it's yet to really come into its own.

Here, the BBC's iPlayer is one of our brighter hopes. The service, which let's you download the last seven days' BBC radio and TV, is slated to offer HD 'soon', although there are concerns that its popularity will prove too much for broadband providers to cope with. ⓖ

DVB-2

The body responsible for deciding what happens to the UK's free HD broadcasting future is Ofcom. Its current stand is that HD will be phased in with the advent of the next digital broadcasting standard DVB-T2, which is based on MPEG-4 rather than the current MPEG-2. This could happen as soon as 2009, although no firm plans have been made as yet.

Introducing disc players

Those shiny little discs are still are great way of getting great content on screen – and Blu-ray makes it HD too

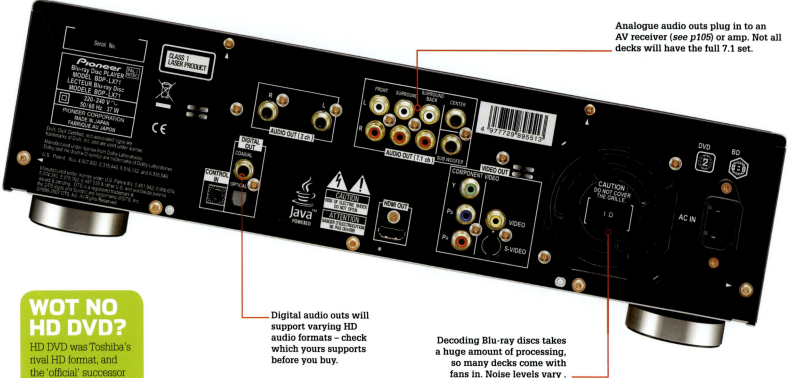

Analogue audio outs plug in to an AV receiver (*see p105*) or amp. Not all decks will have the full 7.1 set.

Digital audio outs will support varying HD audio formats – check which yours supports before you buy.

Decoding Blu-ray discs takes a huge amount of processing, so many decks come with fans in. Noise levels vary .

WOT NO HD DVD?

HD DVD was Toshiba's rival HD format, and the 'official' successor to DVD. Unlike the still-evolving Blu-ray standard, HD DVD's format was more fixed, and many people considered it more elegantly put together. It was also more cost-effective to produce, as it used a similar process to DVD manufacture.

But when Toshiba admitted defeat in March 2008, the price on HD DVD products went through the floor, causing a mass buying spree. While it has no future when it comes to new films or new features, if you want a piece of history (or a cheap DVD upscaler), you should be able to find players for under £75, and a huge range of discs for £5 or less – while stocks last, that is.

T he DVD format was a huge improvement to VHS tapes. But being developed in the early 1990's, when HD video for consumers was still decades away, it's decidedly an SD format.

That's not to say it can't still look great on a great big, modern HDTV, but bear in mind that your beloved movie collection will need help to look its best.

Different TVs will react differently to being fed DVD footage – which contains less than a quarter of the information you'd find in some HD formats – with some making a substantially better fist of it than others. Those with better upscaling capabilities (*see p72*) will try and smooth out the more jagged lines and areas of pixellated detail, whereas other, generally cheaper, sets will just fill in the gaps using basic nearest-neighbour pixels.

In the detail

To sidestep all of that, it's worth avoiding bargain basement DVD players and investing in one that can upscale well at its end. You can then leave the TV to get on with being as honest as possible with all the sources you put into it. We've got two just such devices across the page, which use two different methods to deliver the best possible picture.

After DVD...

There was, until recently, a tussle for our HD attention, as both Toshiba's HD DVD format and Sony's Blu-ray fought to become the de-facto hi-def replacement for DVD (*see left*). After much huffing and puffing, Toshiba finally threw in the towel and Blu-ray now reigns supreme.

But despite all that, prices for both drives and movies remain high – and the technology itself has only recently been finalised. Most issues in older players can be fixed by updating your player's firmware (usually easily done by connecting it to the internet), but some players may not take advantage of new features, and even some new flagship players have quirks that need updating to iron out.

If you're buying a Blu-ray player, check that it at least conforms to the latest HDMI v1.3a standard, as well as its support for BD-Live – an online feature giving access to extras such as unseen footage or mobile phone ringtones. You'll need an internet connection for this too, and some players will also need a memory expansion.

If you want your HD movies on a physical disc, Blu-ray is it. And there's no denying that a decent player with a decent disc and decent TV is a marvel to behold. We've rounded up a pair of the very best on the next page. **iG**

PANASONIC DMP-BD50

Price: £450
Internet: www.panasonic.co.uk
Rating: ★★★★☆

All Blu-ray players are most definitely not equal. This high-spec deck is one of the first to sport the full and final Blu-ray specification, meaning it can deliver multi-stream video playback (picture-in-picture extras, for example) and BD Live internet features. An SD card slot is available for adding extra memory, and there's onboard decoding of Dolby TrueHD and DTS-HD Master Audio, which can be output from the 5.1-channel audio line-outs

There's also Chrome Processing that pulls out an extraordinary amount of detail from discs. Provided your TV can support the 24P mode, it's great to have, and upscaling is also brilliantly achieved for your existing DVD collection. But it's in HD land that it really shines, and if you want the best HD has to offer, you sometimes just have to pay that bit more for it.

SONY BDP-S350

Price: £230
Internet: www.sony.co.uk
Rating: ★★★★☆

First the bad news: with Blu-ray being a barely 'finished' technology, this deck is a reminder of its quirks. While it supports video multi-streaming and BD-Live, you may need to update the firmware to make them work. Secondly, accessing some disc features requires an external, not-included USB memory device. It's just as well that its picture and sound are sensational, then. Pictures display levels of crispness, colour richness and fluid motion that show up much more expensive competition .Sound from Blu-rays, DVDs and CDs could satisfy a high-spec hi-fi system too. The bodywork is a touch flimsy in both look and feel, and we'd ideally like 7.1 analogue audio outs – but in the face of such strikingly affordable AV greatness, any criticisms are little more than HD confetti in the wind.

TOSHIBA XD-E500

Price: £120
Internet: www.toshiba.co.uk
Rating: ★★★★☆

Having seen HD DVD go the way of the dodo, Toshiba now appears hell-bent on sticking a proud two fingers up at the whole HD game. With the home video mass market still DVD-based, this attempt to bring DVDs up to HD standard may catch on. Using a new upscaling processing system dubbed eXended Detail Enhancement, the 'Sharp' upscaling mode delivers picture quality that's unprecedented in the affordable DVD world, all without any artefacts such as glowing edges and blurring.

It still can't make a DVD as sharp, clean and rich as a Blu-ray of the same film, so consider the extra £80 you'd need for an affordable Blu-ray player. But if you've got a huge DVD collection and aren't keen on shelling out for Blu-ray discs, this is one DVD player to absolutely lap up.

SAMSUNG DVD-F1080

Price: £70
Internet: www.samsung.co.uk
Rating: ★★★★☆

A bit of a looker who's also a cheap date? Well, this is currently the finest upscaling DVD player the happy side of £100. And rather than the customary boxiness of of most cheapo DVD decks, this is all glossy curves and cutesy chunkiness, wrapped up in a slinky gloss finish.

Inside beats a heart of pure AV gold, with video processing that's comfortably superior to the vast majority of its competitors: DVDs look sharper, more colourful and less beset by video noise. It also excels at delivering a convincing contrast range and presenting smooth edges. It even plays CDs pretty well. Its only real flaw is making really fast-moving objects a touch blurred, but at this utterly bargain price, we'll let that go.

Upscaling
What it is, how it works

You'll hear a lot about a DVD player or TV's ability to upscale. But what does it actually mean?

1. If it weren't for upscaling, this is all you'd see of a standard DVD picture, but that extra information has to come from somewhere.

2. The first step is to deinterlace the individual fields (shown here) into one progressive frame.

3. Once that's done, the frame can be upscaled, with interpolation making up the gaps

4. Compared to a true 1080p image, the upscaled version won't be as sharp, and some detail may be lacking.

5. An A:B comparison will still reveal differences, but a good upscaler can improve the detail from your DVDs significantly.

DVD was designed to work with the standard-definition TVs that were around when it was introduced in the 1990s. As a result, DVD video is encoded at 576i (or 480i if it's an American disc). Since then, HDTVs capable of displaying 720p, 1080i or 1080p video have been launched into many people's front rooms. And unless you're happy staring at an image that's 576 pixels high, with a huge black border around it, then somewhere along the line the smaller source image needs to be scaled to fit the native resolution of your display. The way this is handled is known as upscaling.

Faking it

Since all HD sets need to handle SD content (as it's still very much the dominant format), they all include the ability to upscale SD to fit the higher resolution of the display. This is done by first deinterlacing the video stream and converting it to a progressive one, since HD sets are progressive by nature. The image is then imbued with extra pixels to make up the higher resolution, which are effectively slotted in between the existing ones. But while you can't magically recreate the actual lost detail, modern upscaling algorithms can be surprisingly effective at taking an educated guess.

Better upscalers, for example, will include more advanced processing to eliminate jagged edges, smooth motion and correct colours. Although all HDTVs include the necessary circuitry to upscale an SD source to fit into an HD resolution (most will downscale, too), they're generally very basic, and an upscaling DVD player will do a much better job outputting directly at 720p, 1080i or 1080p rather than at the normal 576i resolution, without your TV getting involved.

It's important to note, though, that due to the copy protection employed on most commercial DVDs, players will generally only output upscaled images over a protected connection, which means HDMI only – and not the component video that's so common on the rear of players.

Weighing up

Whether a dedicated upscaling DVD player is for you will ultimately come down to personal preference. If you're perfectly happy with how your DVDs look on your HDTV, it may already be doing a good enough job on its own. However, if like most sets at the low- to mid-end, it shows your precious movie collection as being rather fuzzier than you were hoping for, a more advanced DVD player – or a Blu-ray drive that can also upscale standard definition – could be the answer to your prayers. Take a look at p70 for our selection of the best. ◙

Go Green, The Easy Way

The ultimate guide to green living, full of simple steps that will make a difference

Home & Garden • Family & Children • Food & Drink
Work & Office • Transport & Motoring • Fashion & Beauty

Games consoles

The latest games consoles feature stunning HD graphics and sound, but which is best suited to you?

TV and movies are all very good, but when you really want to be involved in the action nothing beats a good video game. The current batch of consoles is just hitting its stride, too, with plenty of big releases on the horizon, all of which you can enjoy on your HDTV. The main contenders for your time and money are Microsoft's Xbox 360 and Sony's PlayStation 3 (PS3), while Nintendo's entertainingly named Wii, although not capable of HD graphics, is an intriguing and highly popular alternative.

Exclusive entertainment
The Xbox 360 launched in the UK in December 2005, over a year ahead of the PS3, which was repeatedly delayed and eventually appeared on shelves in March 2007. The 360's headstart means it has a larger library of games and a a slight edge on exclusive titles for the immediate future. Blockbusters such as *Gears of War* or *Halo 3* may be enough of a swinger for some, but it isn't alone – the thinking man's shooter *BioShock* has been hailed as a modern classic, and racing games such as *PGR 4* are some of the most stunning around: the 360 is certainly the gamers' console of the moment.

The delay in launching the PS3 also cost Sony exclusive titles, with previous PlayStation 2 favourite *Grand Theft Auto* now available on the Xbox and PC as well. And despite much hype, the PS3 has yet to show much technological superiority in its gaming prowess, with major releases (such as EA Sports titles) appearing almost identical on both consoles. Most games run at 720p, with only a handful of simpler games running at 1080p on each console.

Choices, choices
Confusingly, there are three versions of the Xbox 360 on the market, although only the Premium and Elite packages are worthy of your consideration, with the cut-price Arcade package proving a false economy – see our table on the right for the key differences between the top two models. The PS3 has two versions (excluding bundles) in the UK and, although fairly pricey, they're packed full of features.

The Xbox can output HD video over component or VGA, allowing for connection to any PC monitor, while the PS3 comes also with an HDMI port as standard, and can output HD video over component. Both consoles are capable of outputting 720p, 1080i and 1080p, depending on the capabilities of your display. For games, both consoles output Dolby Digital 5.1 surround sound through either an optical S/PDIF or over HDMI.

The Xbox has been plagued with reliability problems since its release, largely stemming from the console overheating. Microsoft claims to have solved these issues now, and so new consoles shouldn't be affected. It's also extended the warranty on all Xbox 360s to three years, so any future problems should be covered. The PS3 hasn't had any hardware issues, and it's also much more quietly cooled than an Xbox, making a low whisper compared to the Xbox's loud fan and disk drive noise.

Bells and whistles
The PS3's key advantage over the Xbox 360 is its built-in Blu-ray optical drive. This means that the PS3 can play HD movies straight out of the box, although you can pick up the ill-fated HD DVD drive add on for the Xbox for about £30.

The Xbox can also act as a Windows Media Center Extender if you have a PC running Media Center (*see p86*), or connect to a Windows PC on the network and access media files. It also has Xbox Live, an established online gaming service for those who want real opponents, although this does require a subscription of £40 a year. The PS3's online service is currently free, although individual developers may charge. The PS3 can also receive streamed media content across a network, has a Freeview tuner option (called PlayTV) and has built-in wireless networking to do so – which you'll have to pay £50 to add to the Xbox.

A Wii alternative
While Microsoft and Sony were fighting for supremacy, Nintendo's Wii snuck in and stole the headlines. Its innovative motion-sensing control system (christened the Wiimote) and easy-to-understand games are a stroke of genius, and prompted a complete sell-out at its launch.

However, software is still relatively thin on the ground, and the bundled *Wii Sports* and Nintendo's *Wii Fit* add-on are still some of the best examples. It's gradually getting better though, particularly as new controllers become introduced – the Nunchuck being a particular favourite.

The Wii is a souped-up version of the Nintendo's previous console, the GameCube, but it doesn't have nearly as much graphical or processing power as the Xbox 360 or PS3. As such, there's no HD capability, with 480p over component being the best available output. Audio is also a step behind, with no digital audio outputs and only Dolby Pro Logic 2 supported. But it makes up for it terms of cuteness.

PC maybe
PCs have been capable of high-resolution graphics and surround sound for some time now. However, with large and often loud tower cases, and games designed to be played using a keyboard and mouse, they've rarely ventured into the living room. Slim media-centre PCs rarely have the space or cooling capability to house hot graphics cards, and you could easily end up spending double what you would on a games console. The advantage for the dedicated gamer is a wide range of titles, and that you can upgrade the graphics card to a more powerful model over time – see p92 for more on your options. Ⓖ

TIP
If you have an older games console kicking about, it's likely you'll find a way of connecting it to your HDTV, even if you have to go through the otherwise rather useless analogue tuner. But prepare yourself for a shock, as those once hi-tech graphics are nakedly revealed by an HD panel.

The big three

MICROSOFT XBOX 360

Still the current favourite with hard-core gamers, but only just. It's rather noisy when running, but once you start playing you're unlikely to notice – or care. The graphics look amazing, with high detail levels and smooth action at 720p. The 360's wireless joypad is arguably the most ergonomic controller around, too, sitting comfortably in the hand for even marathon gaming sessions.

The Xbox Live online service connects you to all your 360-owning chums, so you can keep track of what they're playing, and their gaming achievements, plus easily organise private matches. It's also packed with great downloadable games from arcade classics to addictive German board games and some hidden gems.

The 360 may not have all the frills of the PS3, but it's the games that really matter and, currently, the 360 has a greater variety of high-quality thrills and spills than its competitors.

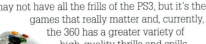

SONY PLAYSTATION 3

The PS3's strength lies in its excellent hardware design with up-to-date features. Weighing an impressive five kilos, with a gloss-black finish, it makes the 360 look rather cheap in comparison. Run the two side-by-side and the PS3 is quieter, cooler and sleeker looking. There's little to tell the two apart when it comes to graphics quality.

The PS3 has an incredible list of features. From the wireless networking, and a BD-Live compatible Blu-ray drive for HD movies, it's a gadget freak's idea of heaven. But it all comes at a cost: the base version costs more than the priciest Xbox 360.

The PS3 has plenty to prove still, with most of its major exclusives limited to Japanese franchises such as *Metal Gear Solid* and *Final Fantasy*, and precious few exclusive titles. But with its PSP handheld console integration, add-ons like the PlayTV tuner and increasingly slick interface, it's an impressive beast to integrate into your HD life.

NINTENDO WII

The tiny Wii may not have the graphical power of the 360 or PS3, but it's the only console that will get your whole family playing video games come Christmas – and for that reason alone it's well worth hooking up to your HD system. The remote-style controller senses the direction and speed of your inputs and translates them accurately into onscreen action. Once you've played *Wii Bowling* or *Wii Tennis* (both included with the console in *Wii Sports*) you'll be hooked, and these simple games will dominate your living room for months after.

The Wii comes with wireless networking, and you can message friends online. Sports titles such as the *FIFA* and the *Madden* series are also available, which allow head-to-head online gaming. Ultimately, the Wii is perfect for occasional gamers, or – better still – as a second console alongside the more hefty HD offerings of the 360 or PS3...

INTRO | CHOOSING | BUYING | SETTING UP | ENJOYING HD | HD ON YOUR PC | EXPANSION | HD HOME

iG Here's how the latest consoles stack up against each other and a typical modern gaming PC.

	Xbox 360 Premium (Elite)	PlayStation 3 (160GB)	Wii	Gaming PC
Price	£170 (£230)	£300 (£340)	£180	£800+
Bundled games	✗	✗	Wii Sports	✗
HD resolutions	720p, 1080i, 1080p	720p, 1080i, 1080p	None (480p supported)	720p, 1080p
Key video outputs	Component, VGA, HDMI	Component, HDMI	Component	HDMI, DVI, VGA
Key audio outputs	Optical S/PDIF, HDMI	Optical S/PDIF, HDMI	Stereo phono	Optical and coaxial S/PDIF
DVD playback	✓	✓	✗	✓
Blu-ray playback	✗	✓	✗	Optional (see p90)
Hard disk	60GB (120GB)	80GB (160GB)	✗	500GB+
Bluetooth	✗	✓	✓	Optional
Memory card reader	✗	✓	SD only	Optional
Vibration feedback controller	✓	✗	✓	✓
Motion-sensing controller	✗	✓	✓	✗
Networking	Wired, optional wireless £55	Wired or wireless	Wireless	Wired or wireless
Online gaming	✓	✓	✓	✓
Media streaming	✓	✓	✗	✓

Blu-ray films

Whether goggling at the quality, or losing yourself in the plot, here are some of the best HD titles to give your TV a good run through

➲ BATMAN: THE DARK KNIGHT

If you're after twisted impact, it's difficult to beat this thrillingly dark tale. Quite aside from the stunning performances of an A-list cast (Christian Bale, Heath Ledger, Morgan Freeman, Gary Oldman) at the height of their powers, there's the astounding scenery, great cinematography and exquisite staging to gawp at. It's two-and-a-half hours of good and evil having a jolly old knees up, before realising that something has gone horribly wrong. If that's not enough for you, the extras are good too, with a decent making-of, and a feature on all those wonderful toys.

➲ BLADE RUNNER: THE FINAL CUT

Ridley Scott's 1982 sci-fi classic provides a rich experience in HD, with the intricate and iconic special effects standing up amazingly well to hi-def scrutiny. Well, as long as you go for the *Final Cut* edition that is, which loses the clangers of the original cut, restoring the film to what it always should have been. You'll find a number of different repackagings, but even the most basic should provide you with some astounding extras, including such delights as 90 mins of deleted scenes and a lovingly made making-of documentary. 5.1 sound and picture quality are top-notch too.

➲ CASINO ROYALE

Daniel Craig's first Bond adventure divided the critics with one of the darkest takes on the franchise yet. But there's no doubting the spectacle this disc offers – from the stomach-twizzling high-rise chase scenes to the sumptuously lit Venetian subterfuge. As one of Sony's showcase Blu-rays, the transfer from film is immaculate, if a little understated in terms of colour. The uncompressed PCM 5.1 soundtrack is stunningly reproduced, though. Most of the Bond movies are now available on Blu-ray, but expect to pick your tongue up from the floor after looking at box set prices.

➲ THE FIFTH ELEMENT

A salutatory lesson in taking notice of exactly what you're buying, as the original Blu-ray release of this absurdly rich visual feast was rather disappointing. Make sure you buy the remastered version, though, and you're in for a real treat, with an AVC MPEG4-encoded, flawless transfer. The audio doesn't disappoint, either, with the Dolby TrueHD soundtrack handling the quirky and hectic soundtrack beautifully. The one disappointment is that the extras are practically non-existent, but when it looks this good, who cares?

➥ FINDING NEMO

Disney's partner in this film, Pixar, was at one point exclusively aligned to the HD DVD camp, so its own films have been a little slow to hit what's now the winning HD disc format. But Disney released this particular fishy tale on Blu-ray early on, and it still looks fantastic now. It's undeniably one of the most beautifully animated features the company has ever produced, as well as being a good bet for just about anyone. Who'd have thought sharks and pelicans would be so funny? Also contains the excellent THX setup video for tweaking your set to perfection.

➥ MONGOL

Regardless of whether Ghengis Khan was a misunderstood military genius or a brutal butcher, there's no denying that this striking first part of his life story does epic in a way that very films manage. Jaw-dropping distance landscape shots, beautifully composed intimate moments and battle scenes that contain more people than old-style TVs have pixels make for a visual treat. The storyline and structure are a bit laboured, certainly, but anyone with a TV over 37in should seriously consider this film on Blu-ray as an exercise in how good HD can look.

➥ PLANET EARTH

It's difficult to find a better showcase for high-definition footage than this astoundingly well-shot series on the world's natural wonders. One of the first major series the BBC shot in HD, you'd be be hard pushed to tell. Whether the camera is sweeping over the world's highest waterfalls, digging around in underwater caves or following insects through the undergrowth, seeing this in HD is a sight to behold. George Fenton's soundtrack is a touch melodramatic at times, but if you like David Attenborough in SD you'll adore him in HD.

➥ TRANSFORMERS

Yes, we thought it was pretty awful, too. But it is *Transformers* and, by turns, somehow manages to be both hilarious and monumental. We can forgive the lack of plot consistency, especially with CGI so good that it isn't hard to suspend your disbelief for two hours – and possibly longer, as you wear out the pause and slow-motion buttons on your remote. Robots that turn into cars, planes and ghetto-blasters they may be, but despite the director's initial protestations, this once HD DVD exclusive has also now transformed into a full-scale Blu-ray release.

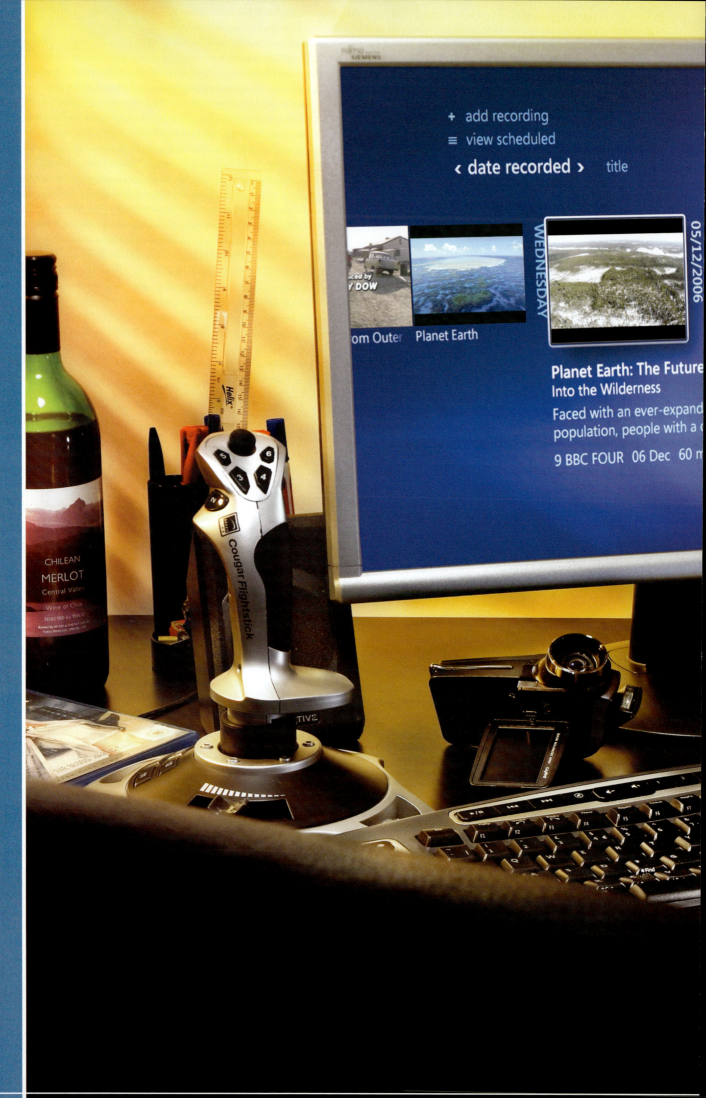

add recording

view scheduled

< date recorded >   title

05/12/2006

WEDNESDAY

om Outer   Planet Earth

Planet Earth: The Future
Into the Wilderness

Faced with an ever-expand
population, people with a c

9 BBC FOUR 06 Dec 60 m

recorded tv

Coyote Ugly   Planet Earth: The Fu   Buffal

r the

22 | 133

I f you have a reasonably modern PC, chances are you have an HD powerhouse sat there ready to go. We'll look at where you can get some stunning HD content online, as well as how you can put the PC at the heart of your HD experience with the latest version of Windows. Banish your confusion as we delve into the murky world of video codecs and the process of adding a TV tuner to your computer. We'll show how to upgrade your crusty old CD-ROM to the latest optical format, before taking alook at the latest generation of stunning high-definition gaming. Time for a sit down...

HD content online

The internet's a great place to find all manner of weird and wonderful footage – some of which is in glorious HD...

LINKS

Planet Earth: www. bbc.co.uk/nature/ animals/planetearth/hd

Sky: http://sky. com/hd/hd-video-downloads.htm

NASA: www.nasa. gov/multimedia/ videogallery/hd_index. html

QuickTime Trailers: www.apple.com/trailers

WMV HD: www.wmvhd.com

Dave's Trailer Page: www.davestrailerpage. co.uk

HD video takes up a lot of space – even lowly 720p-resolution video will occupy around 2GB of disk space per hour, while for 1080p you're looking at around half as much again. Even with today's fast broadband connections, shifting large video files around can feel like the bad old days of slow dial-up connections.

Combine that with the fact that most good content is heavily protected by copyright or DRM, and it's not as easy as we'd like to get HD content. But things are getting better slowly, and you can now find all sorts of features, if not much in the way of full length programmes.

If you enjoyed the BBC's *Planet Earth* programme, for example (and don't want to shell out for the whole series in HD – *see p74*), you'll find some of its highlights available in various forms of high definition. UK TV licence holders can grab them for free by going to the Planet Earth website and choosing the clips that take your fancy.

Sky, keen to push you towards its own satellite HD service, also has clips available so you can see what you're missing out on. Just go to its HD download site for a peek at its high-definition service. If you'd prefer something more educational, the US space agency, NASA, has some stunning footage from its space expeditions in a number of resolutions and formats, all available to download to your PC.

While the US has HD downloads in the iTunes store, for starters, there's no word on when they'll surface in the UK. But you will find an incredible amount of high-definition film trailers available to download. Apple, in particular, has its own dedicated film trailers site, plus an HD showcase, with the content naturally encoded using its QuickTime format. Not to be outdone, though, Microsoft also has a content showcase of its own to display material encoded using its WMV format.

However, if you'd rather skip past the fancy Flash interfaces and marketing fluff, one of our favourites is Dave's Trailer Page (*www.davestrailerpage.co.uk*). It's a remarkably sparse but effective list of links to many film trailers that are available to download. Since there are no affiliations to skew selection, Dave's pages also list everything that's out there, whatever its format, so you can find trailers for the movies you're interested in – a tantalising glimpse of what the future may bring.

As we discover on p84, online HD content is still in its early days, and both downloads and HD VoD (video on demand, that is) will no doubt increase as compression techniques improve and broadband connections become faster. However, there's still plenty out there if you know where to look. 🅖

DRM FAQ...

What is DRM?
➲ DRM, or digital rights management, is technology used to prevent unauthorised use of digital content. If content is protected by DRM then the owner can specify what you can do with it – such as whether you're permitted to make copies or move it from one device to another.

What about copyright?
➲ Copyright is separate from DRM, giving the creator of a piece of work the exclusive right to make copies of it. Prior to the digital revolution, any unauthorised reproductions would be inferior to the original – for example, copies of tapes had more hiss on them than the original. With digital content, however, it's possible to make an exact duplicate without any degradation – DRM is used to prevent anyone but the creator of the work doing so, thus protecting the terms of the copyright.

If I've bought the content, shouldn't I be able to do what I want with it?
➲ No, you've only bought a licence to view or listen to the content in the format it was sold. The original owner still holds the copyright and hasn't necessarily granted you permission to make further reproductions, even if they're only for your personal use.

What types of content can DRM be applied to?
➲ DRM can be used with any type of digital content, be it audio, video or documents. However, it's most widely used with music and video. The video industry is slightly behind the music industry, mainly because take-up of digital video has been slower due to the bigger file sizes involved and fewer ubiquitous file formats, but it's slowly catching up.

Will video be offered DRM-free, like the unprotected audio tracks you can get on iTunes?
➲ Whether content is available without DRM protection is ultimately down to the holder of the copyright. The music industry is more advanced in digital distribution, so while it's likely that any progress made there may influence the video market, there are no guarantees.

Do DVDs include DRM?
➲ DVDs are protected by a rights management system called CSS (Content Scrambling System) that encodes the content so it can only be played back on authorised devices. However, it was defeated some time ago by a chap called Jon Lech Johansen (also, incidentally, known as DVD Jon) while he was trying to create a DVD player application for the Linux operating system. Subsequently, the code has been used by numerous other developers to easily decrypt all commercial DVDs, although it's generally considered illegal to use such applications.

What about Blu-ray?
➲ Blu-ray discs use a more advanced form of copy protection called AACS (Advanced Access Content System), which supposedly improves on many of the flaws in CSS. However, some parts of AACS have also been compromised, making it possible to extract data from some Blu-ray discs and remove the DRM protection.

What about online video?
➲ Online video can also be protected by DRM, such as video files distributed in Microsoft's WMV format. Although you can freely copy and download files that have been encoded in this way, they require a key to enable playback. Depending on the type of DRM, you'll be limited to the number of times you can play a file, or to a specific timeframe to watch it in. For example, programmes downloaded with the BBC's iPlayer application are in protected WMV format. Once you've downloaded a programme, you have 30 days to watch it. And, once you start watching it, you have only seven days to finish viewing it before the key expires.

Is it possible to convert DRM-protected content from one format to another?
➲ Not without removing the DRM protection first. This could present a problem if you have a media device that can play back one format, but your content is in another. Unfortunately, there's little you can do in this situation to view the content, other than look for a compatible version.

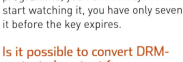

The internet and on-demand content

On-demand HD content may seem like just a dream but major broadcasters are already offering a taste of the future

The days of sitting in your pyjamas, passively letting TV wash over you, are coming to an end – if you believe the hype. No, instead of watching linear, scheduled TV services, soon we'll all be choosing what we want to watch, available to view at the click of button, whenever we please.

This change is all possible thanks to the PC revolution, and the marvel of broadband: with advancements in compression technology, video can now be streamed over the internet in real-time at decent quality, albeit not routinely in high definition. There are a couple of stumbling blocks to contend with before we get there, however. Despite speed increases and clever compression techniques, HD content is still very data-intensive to transfer reliably, hence the rise of standalone cable boxes (see p66).

Second, if you start downloading large video files, you could end up with a big bandwidth bill or your ISP may even suspend your internet connection. Some broadband providers impose download limits as low as 1GB a month – barely enough for three hours of standard-definition TV. Before starting to use a download service, it's important to know what limits there are on your account. Even supposed unlimited connections allow the ISP to suspend your connection if you contravene its so-called fair-usage policy by downloading too much.

There are two main types of service currently available – catch-up facilities that allow you to download programmes to watch for a certain amount of time after they were broadcast (typically, seven to 14 days), and on-demand

services that mimic live TV and allow you to access content immediately without having to download it first.

Playing catch-up

There's currently no equivalent to Freeview when it comes to online video – each broadcaster has its own program you need to download if you want to access its content. The BBC, ITV and Channel 4 are apparently working on a joint platform dubbed 'Project Kangaroo', which would enable users to download the programmes of their choice via the same interface, but it's still early days and there's no guarantee that it will come to anything.

Channel 4 was the first UK broadcaster to offer a download service with 4oD (*www.channel4.com/4od*), which launched in December 2006. It's available to UK residents only, and you'll need to install the 4oD application to access it. Programmes are downloaded via peer-to-peer file sharing and are protected so they can only be watched on the machine on which they were downloaded. In addition, content is time-limited, so you have to watch it within a particular timeframe before it expires. The majority of content is free, although you'll have to pay for some films or US imports.

The BBC started developing what is now its iPlayer application (*www.bbc.co.uk/iplayer*) in 2003, but it only became available generally in June 2007. Like 4oD, it requires you to install an application that downloads programmes from a peer-to-peer network (effectively, other users of the service) and content is tied to the

> ## "Despite the compression techniques, HD content is too data intensive to transfer reliably"

machine from which it was downloaded, as well as being time-limited. All content is currently free to access for UK TV licence holders.

Channel 5 has a limited download service (*http://download.five.tv*), which sells episodes of mainly US programmes for between £1.50 and £2.50 each. There's no software to install; just download the episodes you've paid for – they're tied to the PC you downloaded them on, but there's no time limit.

Sky also has a download facility (*http://anytime.sky.com*), accessible by subscribers to its satellite TV service. Content is downloaded via a peer-to-peer network and protected by DRM. The programmes available vary depending on the level of your satellite subscription.

Streaming on-demand

ITV doesn't have a download service, but does provide catch-up episodes of its popular programmes online (*www.itv.com*). There's no charge for watching them, but you do have to sit through adverts first and the resolution is low even compared to standard-definition TV. It's the only UK TV station currently able to stream programmes without having to download them, though.

However, there are other options available if you'd prefer something a bit more spontaneous. Joost (*www.joost.com*), created by the same people who developed the popular Skype and Kazaa programs, is a free video service that combines peer-to-peer downloads with near-instant access. You need to install the Joost application and log in, after which you can browse through the 40-odd channels available. Programmes are delivered on-demand, so if you don't like the one you're currently watching you can just skip to the next one.

Given that programmes are being streamed, rather than downloaded in advance, the quality is impressive – around the same as standard-definition TV. However, you'll need to give it the bulk of your broadband connection if you want playback to be seamless. Joost is also free and there's some decent content on there, such as classic movies from Paramount like *Breakfast at Tiffany's* or *Fatal Attraction*, for example. You do have to watch advertisements, but not that many – during a typical movie, you'll probably only be shown three or four adverts.

Livestation (*www.livestation.com*) is another video service – one that Microsoft has had a hand in developing, although it's currently a limited beta test. As such, you'll need to sign up and wait for an invitation before you're able to try it out. Livestation offers broadcast channels, rather than on-demand content. The quality is fairly limited at the moment, but its developers are hoping to improve this in the future. With some big friends behind it, it's a promising technology and could well be worth watching. Quite literally. Ⓖ

Illustration: Linda Duong

Using Windows Media Center

Windows Vista includes a powerful interface for accessing your digital music, photos and recording TV. It's time to press the green button...

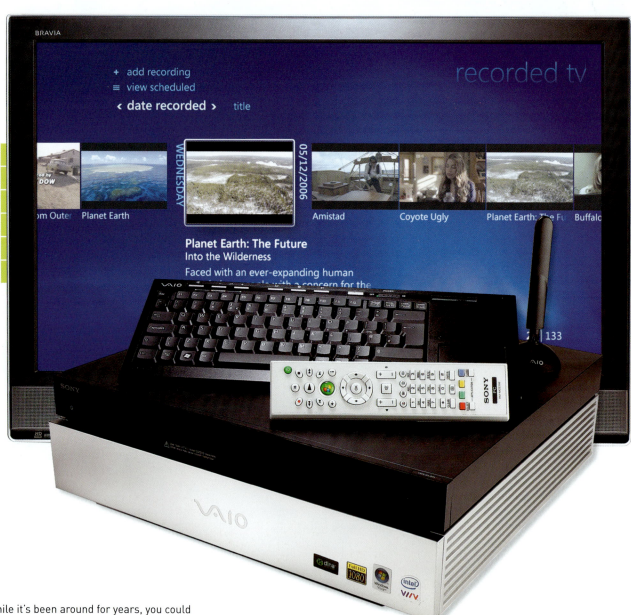

While it's been around for years, you could be forgiven for not coming across Windows Media Center before. For much of that time it's been hidden away in the Media Center Edition of Windows XP, which you could only get on new PCs (or in a roll-your-own version best left for masochists). Now, though, it comes as part of the two main retail versions of Windows Vista: the Home Premium and Ultimate Editions. If you're a music, video or TV fan, it could be reason enough to upgrade. If you're feeling ambitious, you could even opt for a dedicated media-centre PC for your living room, like the one above.

⊙ Main Menu

Media Center's interface works like a grid, with options above, below and to either side of the main list. This makes it easy to navigate with a remote control. It takes advantage of widescreen displays if you've got one, and once you've worked it out it's surprisingly intuitive. You can get back to this menu at any point by pressing the green Media Center button, either on the remote or with your mouse. You'll see this button ever-present, in the top left or right corner, just about everywhere you go in the program.

⊙ Picture/video library

In a similar vein to the music library, both the picture and video libraries use tiled thumbnail previews spread horizontally across the screen. Here, though, you can browse by folder, date shot (using data from your digital camera) or by tag (metadata you've added yourself). This last option makes it worth spending a little time adding tags to your photos, as it makes them so much quicker to find. See p44 for more on tagging your media.

⊙ Music library

Once Media Center has scanned your music folders, it presents your music as a series of album covers along the central strip of the screen. Scrolling left and right, you can browse the whole library, or just start typing to do an instant search. You can switch between two sizes of cover artwork, or show everything as a text list if you prefer. Going up to the next level of the menu and scrolling left or right, you can sort by album, artist, genre, song, composer or year. When you've found what you want, you can either start it playing straight away or add it to a queue.

⊙ Online

Essentially, it's a portal where you can access websites that are specially adapted for the Media Center interface. You could find anything springing up here, from a pay-per-track karaoke service to sporting highlights or movie downloads. Particular favourites include the on-demand BBC News player, which offers headline-related video clips and full TV programmes that can be streamed in real-time to your PC. Even if there's nothing here for you now, it's worth coming back occasionally to see if anything new has been added.

The DVD generation

In late 2001, when Windows XP was released, DVD films still accounted for only the minority of the market, and you couldn't even watch them in Windows without using extra software. In Windows Vista, DVD playback is built in – there's an MPEG-2 decoder as standard, so you can play DVD movies on your PC straight away.

The inclusion of that decoder also means that Media Center can handle analogue or digital (DVB-T) broadcasts without fuss, something that often caused problems in Windows XP. You'll need TV tuner hardware in your PC (see p88), but it needn't be difficult to install and you'll often get an FM tuner into the bargain, too. Sadly, there's currently no Media Center support for Freesat tuners.

Flexible friend

As the Media Center interface is specialised for viewing photographs, music and video, it isn't like most other Windows programs: you won't find fiddly drop-down menus or hundreds of settings. In fact, with its mix of bold text

and thumbnail pictures, it isn't like using Windows at all. It's equally at home sitting discreetly on your desktop while you're working with a keyboard and mouse, or running full-screen in conjunction with a remote control and your sofa. You can do a surprising amount within the interface, too: archiving video, burning compilation CDs, synchronising with an MP3 player, or even accessing the internet or playing games – all from just your remote control.

While Media Center is impressively flexible in its basic state, the real advantage of doing all this on your PC – rather than using something like a Sky+ box – is that you can extend its features. If you have more than one computer, you can use network attached storage (see p124) to deliver the same experience on each. Or you can use Media Center Extender devices (or an Xbox 360 – see p72) to stream the interface in all its glory to up to five screens anywhere around the house.

You can even integrate Media Center into a home automation system and use it to control your lighting or security system. Ⓖ

Using your TV as a PVR

You can use your PC as a PVR, with with features that easily outrival standalone units – and at a fraction of the cost

Even if you're convinced there's nothing worth watching on TV these days, chances are there's something on every now and then, or in the wee hours of the morning that will pique your interest. And if you don't have the time to stare at whatever happens to be on, the features at the heart of Windows Media Center (*see p86*) could be just what you're looking for.

With a combination of sophisticated search facilities, support for multiple tuners and the flexibility to take recordings away with you on a portable device, you can skim off just what you want to watch, regardless of what time or channel it's on. It's TV for the 21st century. Adding a second tuner allows you to do even more: you can record two programmes at once (while still being able to watch a third, recorded programme), or watch a different channel while another records.

The guide

Whether you're watching live or recorded TV, you can pause or rewind it, browse what's on now and next, or bring up a full-screen grid view – all with the picture carrying on behind it. You can also filter what's on offer using categories to see at a glance what's on over the following fortnight. Every day, Media Center will download 15 days of advance listings for each channel you can receive.

There's no need to mess around with timers: use the Guide to browse, or use the search facilities (*see below*) to find something you might be interested in later. Then, just press Record and Media Center will kick into action when the time comes. If you want to record a series, press the button again and it will record every episode with no further intervention. If your power options are set correctly, Media Center will automatically wake up your PC, record the programme and then shut it down again. The next time you come to it, the recordings will be sitting on your hard disk waiting for you. You can also skip through adverts, drag off a programme to a laptop or portable hard disk, burn it onto a DVD for backup (*see p97*), or watch it from another PC on your network.

Discover a channel

Using the Search option in the main menu (or from Recorded TV), you can scour the TV listings by title, keyword or category. Programme descriptions are catalogued, so you can try the keyword search, or use it to find programmes featuring specific actors or directors. Category search enables you to browse by categories such as sport, documentaries or children's, or follow these through to anything from cricket to gardening and sitcoms. There's a film section, too, showing all the movies for the next fortnight.

TIP

Recording TV is very demanding of disk space. It isn't a big problem with today's large hard disk capacities, but an hour of TV takes up to 2GB, so older PCs may soon feel the strain. Media Center will warn you in advance if there isn't enough spare storage, but you can switch the recording location to an external or network disk, and limit the space available for it to ensure there's enough for everything else you need on your PC. You can also set recordings to auto-expire (oldest first) when the space is needed or as soon as they're watched.

Add recording allows you to search for upcoming TV to record.

View scheduled shows you TV that's due to record, as well as any upcoming conflicts that need dealing with.

Sort recordings by date or title; episodes from a series will be grouped together. Or search your recordings by typing a title.

Search for a keyword to instantly see relevant programmes.

A thumbnail of each recording appears with the date recorded on the edge and the title below. The current focus shows more info.

These figures show where you are (7) within the total number of recordings in your library (148).

How to...
add a TV tuner

Many new PCs (and even notebooks) now come with TV tuners built in, but it isn't difficult to add one to an existing system. If you've already got a single tuner, you can use this method to install a second one

1 Select a TV tuner

In the UK, Media Center has a choice between analogue, hybrid and digital (DVB-T) tuners. The former can receive the five terrestrial channels, but it's better to opt for a hybrid or digital tuner – these give you the 70-odd channels of Freeview TV and radio through your aerial (*www.freeview.co.uk*). Hybrid means it includes both an analogue and digital tuner. You can opt for an internal card or a USB version. Whichever you choose, make sure its drivers are compatible with Media Center, and install it after upgrading your PC to Vista if you're doing so.

2 Load the drivers

Before you've installed your internal PCI card or plugged in your USB tuner, make sure you have the right drivers downloaded from the manufacturer's website (or use the supplied disc). Then try running the installation software: if it says it can't find the device, turn off your PC and plug it in now, or it may install before asking you to power down and plug in the tuner. Switch the PC back on and it should install everything it needs. Start up Media Center and go to the 'set up TV' option on the TV level of the menu, or go to Settings, TV, Set up TV signal.

3 Set up TV channels

Media Center will hold your hand for a while here: each step is preceded by an introduction screen, which you should read and click through. You'll need to confirm your region (it should be set to UK), confirm the tuners you want to use, then agree to the Guide terms and conditions. Finally, you'll enter your postcode and set your nearest signal provider, which you'll need to check yourself. Eventually, you'll get to scanning for the services you can receive. If you haven't already connected your rooftop or indoor aerial, now would be the time.

4 See what you've got

How many services you get will very much depend on the quality and positioning of your aerial, as well as the signal strength available in your area. Once you're finished setting up, you'll see the Live TV and Guide options appear in the Media Center menu. Check the Guide for the full line-up, which will also contain all the Freeview digital radio channels. Note that all the screenshots we've used here are from Vista's Media Center, but the version in Windows XP works in a very similar way.

Playing HD discs on your PC

You can make your computer into an HD haven with the simple addition of a Blu-ray drive and a small helping of software...

While under-the-TV players are great for watching films, the PC offers more than just stunning video playback. As with DVDs when they first arrived on the scene, Blu-ray drives in PCs and notebooks have even greater potential, allowing you not only to watch films, but also to burn your own discs.

HD video contains far more data than that on DVDs, which is why new optical disc formats were needed in the first place. But that also means you can use that extra capacity for data storage and backups for music, photos or video. Here's a selection of the latest drives and, on the opposite page, some of the software available for playback and burning the new generation of discs.

Do it yourself

Before you do upgrade your PC, there are a few things to check. If it's more than a couple of years old, it may simply not be fast enough to cope with decoding the huge amount of data needed. If you've got a a dual (or quad) core processor, you should be okay, but older (or budget) single core processors like AMD Athlon XP or Intel Pentium 4 models will struggle.

Your graphics card will also need to be relatively modern – both to offer a digital DVI-type output (*see p38*) and to support HDCP (High Definition Content Protection) in order to successfully output it to a digital screen which, it should go without saying, be at the very least HD ready, as big as possible and itself HDCP compliant.

You'll also need to ensure that you've got a spare bay to put the drive in. Most larger 'tower' PCs will have at least one, but a smaller media centre chassis or compact desktop may already be fully stocked with an existing DVD player. Check for blanking plates near the drive that's already there for a clue. If you're adding a drive, you should also check whether you have a spare S-ATA interface connector and power cable from your computer's supply – highly likely in both cases, but better safe than sorry.

Installation

Hooking your drive up should be a few minutes' screwdriver work in most cases (literally), but the specifics will vary. Once the power's off, take off the side of the case and take a peek inside. There's often a cage to house optical drives, which needs to be removed before you can slot the Blu-ray player in and secure it with screws. In some cases, you'll need to take off a panel at the front, before attaching rails and sliding it back in. You can then attach the data and power cables, making sure to avoid touching the motherboard at all times. If you can't face all that, or your not sure of what you're doing – go for an external model.

⬆ LG GGW-H20L

Price	**£165**
Internet	**www.lge.co.uk**
Rating	★★★★☆

Costing around three times this much until recently, prices have now reached the not-so-silly level. The end of the HD DVD / Blu-ray format war may make buying an HD drive less of a gamble, but this drive will actually read both formats anyway. It will only write to Blu-ray discs, which are still pretty pricey – but we're not complaining when many more expensive drives only read either HD format.

It even writes to dual-layer format discs, giving up to 50GB of storage, or half that on a single layer disc. If you can find 4x discs, it'll take about an hour to fill up a 50GB disc – hardly convenient next to hard drives, but if you're shooting your own HD video, it's a useful option.

It's also a fully functioning CD and DVD writer, and burns to these media at decent speeds too – a DVD in about six minutes, and a CD in less than 60 seconds at full speed. There's support for dual-layer DVDs too (holding 8GB), but it's the one area we found the drive actively sluggish. All told, though, this is a great value way of bringing your PC kicking and screaming into the HD revolution.

⮯ LITEON DX-4012-03C

Price	£126
Internet	www.liteonit.com
Rating	★★★★☆

For those without the time, inclination or skills to venture into their computer's innards with confidence, it's reassuring to know that there's another way. This drive connects via a USB cable, so there's no need to even search for a screwdriver – just a spare port and a power socket.

Unlike the LG (*opposite*), this is strictly a disc reader – it doesn't write to either of the HD formats or, indeed, even to the humble CD and DVD. But it will read any modern format you give it – except HD DVD, which is no great loss unless you've already got a big library of them.

As with any Blu-ray drive, you'll need software to get Windows XP or Vista to decode and play back discs, and this comes with a version of Cyberlink's *PowerDVD* thrown in.

The lack of writing features isn't terminal for most people, and for those with several PCs or small or complex cases, it's an instant Blu-ray fix. It's also a good option if you want to add HD disc playback to a suitably powerful notebook computer, as it's relatively portable.

⮯ CYBERLINK POWERDVD ULTRA

Price	£53
Internet	www.cyberlink.com
Rating	★★★★★

CyberLink PowerDVD Ultra comes with an array of support for HD formats. It will do pretty much anything you'd expect of normal DVD playback software, such as bookmarking options and some very swish interactive menus.

It won't burn discs, but it can play H.264, MPEG2 and WMV-HD formats, as well as DivX Pro, mini-DVD and standard DVDs. It supports hardware acceleration to make full use of your PC's graphics card, and will also cope with interactive features via BD-Live.

Watching a director's commentary in picture-in-picture mode during the film brings new life to the added extras, and PowerDVD also performs clever tricks such as subtly speeding up playback if it detects a laptop battery is running out, and moving subtitles to the black bars so they don't obstruct the screen. The interface is great, image quality is top-notch and, with support for Dolby Digital Plus, TrueHD and DTS audio, it's an excellent choice to make your PC a fully fledged Blu-ray player.

⮯ ROXIO CREATOR 2009

Price	£50
Internet	www.roxio.co.uk
Rating	★★★★☆

Although it supports playback of Blu-ray, this package is so much more than just a player. There's support for Dolby Digital EX 6.1 and 5.1 output, plus Pro Logic and Dolby Headphone. It also has what it calls a VGA Optimizer built in, to make keep graphics settings under control.

It can burn to Blu-ray (for a £15 upgrade), and the Copy utility can duplicate them as well, as long as they don't have copy protection (so no commercial movies, sadly).

The Drag and Drop convertor is a particular godsend when it comes to converting video, audio or photos for portable devices too. This latest version adds support for AVCHD camcorders (*see p134*), and there's even a basic video editor built in. It also handles the transcoding of files to and from mobile devices, it can upload videos to YouTube and throws in some handy audio features too. It's difficult to argue with the sheer number of utilities bundled in here and although the power doesn't match dedicated applications, it's an incredibly useful package.

⮯ NERO 9

Price	£50
Internet	www.nero.com
Rating	★★★★★

Although it doesn't have the sheer number of features that Roxio's suite has, Nero 9 has a much neater interface, and is better at disc-authoring. Its StartSmart interface gives direct access to basic tools for burning data and audio discs, ripping audio and disc copying. Plus, you can customise buttons along the top for quick access to favourite tasks.

It's still incredibly flexible, even offering PVR features if you have a TV tuner installed, and other tasks integrate well with Vista, with Sidebar gadgets for drag-and-drop authoring and simple disc copying. It can burn to Blu-ray and HD DVD, import from AVCHD camcorders and, like Roxio, upload videos easily to YouTube. There's even a feature that claims to rescue files from damaged discs.

It may not be as dedicated to the viewing of high-definition entertainment as CyberLink's software, and it isn't as jam-packed with features as Roxio 10, but for its range of useful disc-authoring options and its organised interface Nero 8 is well worth the asking price.

Graphics cards

It's a complicated business, but the right graphics card will give a stunning HD experience

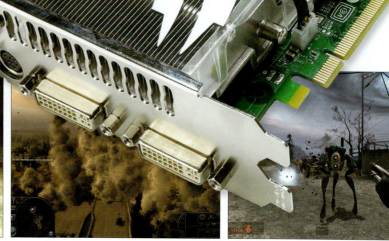

Your PC already has some kind of graphics processor in it: if it didn't, there'd be nothing to plug your screen into. But depending on what's in there already, getting high-definition content from your PC to a shiny new HDTV may require some more advanced hardware to offload the strain from your main processor to the graphics card.

High-definition video is very intensive for a PC, and a decent graphics card will make a difference to smooth playback, particularly if you want your PC to get on with another task in the background. For 1080p, you'll need a fast processor for it to work well (say, a 3GHz Pentium 4 or 2GHz Core 2 Duo. 1080i and 720p formats should prove less of a problem, though.

What to look for

A good HDTV will also make modern games look stunning, but you'll need a higher-end card for it. You can buy cards for about £30 at the bottom of the market, but their 3D performance is minimal. If you want to play modern games (see p94), you'll need a card more in the mid-range, costing you between £70 and £100. These will give you smooth gaming performance on most titles. If you want to play the latest and greatest games on your PC, though, you should budget for about twice that, besides ensuring that your PC's processor is up to the job.

The most important specification to watch for when buying a new graphics card is that it supports HDCP (see p38). If it doesn't, you could well find yourself with a graphics card incapable of decoding encrypted Blu-ray discs. Don't get overly concerned if your card doesn't have an HDMI connector, though: a standard DVI converter can be compatible with HDCP (all the cards featured opposite are), and an HDMI converter will set you back just over £10.

For gaming and HD support, the latest generation of cards are the only ones worth investing in – that means DirectX 10 support for games and some form of HD acceleration capabilities. Check these are on offer before buying.

Executive decision

The graphics card market is dominated by two major players – ATi and Nvidia. It's worth doing some research before you spend any money, since many graphics cards have decent games bundled with them, too.

To get your PC to play high-definition content, you'll obviously need a Blu-ray drive for your computer as well (see p90), most of which will come with some form of playback software – most graphics cards don't, however. Graphics cards also aren't supplied with the H.264 codec needed for lots of HD content (see p96), so make sure it's present with the software accompanying your optical drive.

ATi cards also come with Avivo technology, which improves video playback performance. It also has a positive effect on image quality, particularly when it comes to smoothing edges and upscaling (see p72). Nvidia cards, on the other hand, don't come with any software – if you want Nvidia's PureVideo software, which offers similar features to Avivo, you'll be looking at a bill of between £10 and £25, depending on the outputs. Technically speaking, PureVideo offers less impressive technical quality than Avivo, but from normal viewing distances either is fine.

It's tempting to spend as much as you can on a graphics card – not only will you get good performance immediately, but you'll also get a card that plays new games well into the future. However, there are some important considerations. Shifting all those gaming pixels around the screen is heavy work, and graphics cards require plenty of cooling.

This results in noise: top-end cards come with large fans that whirr away; many are audible even when the card isn't doing any gaming work. Expensive graphics cards also come with power requirements beyond the reach of many media-centre PCs, so make sure your power supply can handle it before splashing out, and check what power connections you have spare. If all you want is a card that can render high-definition video with no fuss (and not so much games), it's best to opt for one of the less spectacular, but quieter, models featured opposite. **Ⓖ**

PCI EXPRESS

If your PC is more than a few years old, it's likely to have an old-style AGP slot, rather than the more modern PCI Express interface. That's not the end of the world, since you can still get recent cards in an AGP version, but it's likely that the rest of the PC's components will be borderline when it comes to playing modern games.

⮀ XFX GEFORCE 8400 GS

Price:	Around £20
Internet:	www.nvidia.co.uk
Rating:	★★★★☆

The GeForce 8400 GS is a great way to get high-definition playback on a tiny budget. It uses Nvidia's dedicated PureVideo HD decoder, which helps decode Blu-ray discs and other high-def sources, so you don't need a top-flight CPU to watch HD movies. And with the bundled adapter its DVI socket can connect directly to any HDMI-equipped TV or projector, conveying sound as well as video.

What's more, thanks to the low-power design, it doesn't need a fan to keep cool. That means there's zero noise to interfere with your movie-watching experience – ideal for a media PC in your living room or home cinema. DirectX 10 compatibility means modern games will run, although you'll have to turn the settings right down in most of them.

⮀ SAPPHIRE RADEON HD 4670

Price:	Around £60
Internet:	ati.amd.com
Rating:	★★★★★

Its name may be a bit of a mouthful, but the ATI Radeon HD 4670 is a highly efficient little card. Like the 8400 GS, its DVI output will connect to any HDMI TV or projector. And, it also has a built-in hardware HD decoder – in this case, ATI's Unified Video Decoder. It's a more powerful system than Nvidia's, so you can get away with a budget CPU. And it'll upscale DVDs to look great on your HD display.

The HD 4670 is also more powerful than the GeForce when it comes to 3D gaming: *Crysis*, for example, runs happily at 720p with medium lighting and shading effects. The card has a small fan, so it's not quite silent, but if you want to play the odd game as well as watching movies, it's a great value option.

⮀ SAPPHIRE RADEON HD 4850

Price:	Around £105
Internet:	ati.amd.com
Rating:	★★★★★

The Radeon HD 4850 is the HD 4670's big brother. It has all the same HD video features, including HDMI compatibility and the same Unified Video Decoder technology to play Blu-ray discs and upscale DVDs. Under the bonnet, however, it's a much beefier beast. It has more than twice the processing power, meaning it makes short work of 3D games. The most demanding modern titles become very playable, even at full HD, 1080p resolution.

It's also a good choice if you're interested in authoring your own videos. Software such as Cyberlink PowerDirector can harness its power to speed up video encoding. According to ATI's figures, creating a Blu-ray video with this is 19 times faster than with a modern CPU on its own. Beyond this price tag, you'll get diminishing returns.

⮀ MSI N280GTX-T2D1G

Price:	Around £270
Internet:	www.nvidia.com
Rating:	★★★★☆

If you're serious about image quality, the GTX 280 is where it's at. The price tag is enormous, but it buys you a phenomenal amount of processing power. With a card like this, you can play more or less any game at 1080p resolution with all the bells and whistles. So there.

Needless to say, you also get HDMI support, along with Nvidia's PureVideo HD decoder and all the benefits that entails. And with the free Badaboom (yes, really) video encoder you can transcode video at super-speed – Nvidia claims a seven-fold speed increase over a CPU alone. Just note that if you do splash out, you'll need a mighty power supply: Nvidia recommends your PC should have at least a 550W PSU, and it'll need both 8-pin and 6-pin internal connectors to power the card. Whoosh.

93

Great PC games for HD

There are plenty of reasons to hook an HD-capable display to your PC – but next-generation gaming has to be one of the most exciting

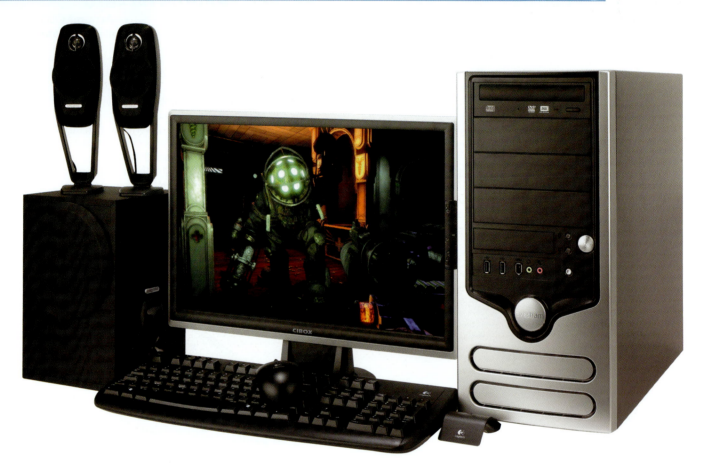

Game on: Whether on your desk or connected to your TV, the humble PC is a cracking HD games platform.

Half-Life 2

It may be a couple of years old now, but this is still a mighty fine game. And if you have even a modest modern card, you'll be able to play it at full HD with all the bells and whistles switched on. A spooky police force that's clamping down on people's movements doesn't stop you roaming the countryside, battling zombies and stumbling across some astonishing scenery. Brilliantly paced throughout and perfectly balanced between taxing and rewarding, *Half-Life 2* is a game you'll keep coming back to. Look out for the bridge-scaling section, which will have you sitting on the edge of your seat.
➲ **www.valvesoftware.com**

Flight Simulator X

Microsoft's flight simulator should be at the top of every wannabe pilot's shopping list. This is the best version yet, with the most notable inclusion being some incredible graphics: rain clouds reflect off the runway and you share the virtual world with all manner of moving traffic – other planes, cars on highways and even schools of dolphins.

A huge variety of scenery swishes beneath you – high-resolution houses and smoking factories, as well as real-life roads to help you navigate without needing GPS. There are 24 planes to fly, and more than 50 missions for those who want to start learning to fly from scratch. Neeeeeeeooooooooooow, now in HD.
➲ **www.microsoft.com**

Bioshock

This isn't just a great first-person shooter but it's quite a work of art, too, making it a real treat when played on high-definition equipment. The art director's vision is evident in every grand hall or submerged corridor of the game's undersea city setting. Wrapped in art-deco-style 1930s fashions, it's one of the most sumptuous worlds ever seen in a PC game and will haunt you from the moment you enter it. Whether it's hitting you with chilling encounters or moments of stomach-churning realisation, it will make you think, reflect and feel. For once, the hype is right. Just don't have nightmares.
➲ **www.2kgames.com**

HALF-LIFE 2

CRYSIS

FLIGHT SIMULATOR X

FIFA 2009

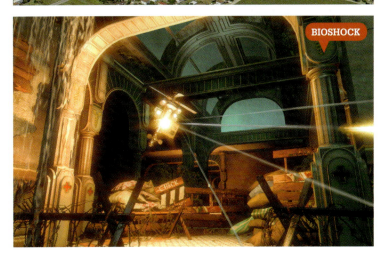

BIOSHOCK

RACEDRIVER: GRID

Crysis

One of the first games to really take advantage of the latest DirectX 10 technology, Crysis is a jaw-dropping follow-up to the hugely popular *Far Cry* – a fabulous title in its own right. It takes interactivity to a new level, with bushes that move when you brush past them, trees that you can hack to pieces realistically, and physics so real you'll feel like you're there. The plot isn't complex, but the gameplay is ridiculously engrossing, whether you're on a mission or just kicking objects around to see what they do. Play this on the big screen, and you'll practically feel the mosquitos buzzing around your ears.

↪ www.ea.com/crysis

FIFA 2009

After seasons of quibbling over which is the best footy title (*Pro Evolution* or *FIFA*), EA's latest run-out could be the best we've ever seen. Gloriously lush detail from atmospheric stadiums right down to perfectly colour-saturated blades of grass and realistic player mapping score highly. Bountiful game modes sees the usual exhibition line up alongside the fantastic Be a Pro Mode, Manager mode, as well as Adidas Live updating player stats from real-world information. Gameplay is quicker, computer opponents and team mates show a hitherto unseen level of intellect and physics make tackles and jostling for balls so real you'll be reaching for the magic sponge.

■ www.fifa09.ea.com

Racedriver: GRID

Revving up the graphics engine of *Colin McRae: DIRT*, Codemasters puts pedal to the metal with a racer that's enough to have wannabe Schumachers steaming up their visors. Work up the ranks on beautifully rendered street tracks from around the world, or jump start the demolition derby mode to ignite extra excitement. Cars handle smoothly, if a bit over-enthusiastically, and look stunning, with light and environments reflecting off bodywork. Damage modelling affects car performance and gives it the realism others lack. The raciest HD experience around, no driving fan should miss out on.

↪ www.racedrivergrid.com

HD ON YOUR PC

INTRO | CHOOSING | BUYING | SETTING UP | ENJOYING HD | HD ON YOUR PC | EXPANSION | HD HOME

www.igizmo.co.uk   The Ultimate Guide to HDTV

Video codecs

If you're interested in online video or HD, you'll hear the word 'codec' often. We reveal what they are and how they work

WHERE TO GET YOUR CODECS

You'll find a lot of websites promising all sorts of codecs online, but stick to these and you shouldn't go far wrong.

- **DivX** www.divx.com
- **XviD** www.xvid.org
- **MPEG-4 H.264/AVC** www.cccp-project.net
- **WMV** www.microsoft.com/windowsmedia

Video data consumes an immense amount of space, and that's particularly true when it comes to high-definition footage. With each 1080p frame effectively an image measuring 1920 x 1080 pixels, just one uncompressed frame would occupy around 6MB. Multiply that by 25 frames a second and you're looking at a whopping 9GB for every minute of footage – and that's before you consider the audio. So, in order to make the volume of data manageable, compression is employed to reduce it to a more manageable amount.

To compress the data you need a codec (an encoder / decoder) – a computer algorithm used to remove unnecessary information and reduce the overall file size. In order to play back the file, the computer needs to perform the same procedure in reverse, expanding the compressed data back to its original size before displaying it onscreen. Codecs can either be lossless, which preserves all the original data, or lossy, which discards data during the compression process. Although it's possible to use lossless codecs with video, the volume of data is still so big that generally only lossy codecs are employed. Different codecs handle video in different ways, resulting in varying compression levels and quality. You can tell when too much compression has been used when visible 'artefacts' appear, particularly in scenes with high dynamic range, or on gradiated colours such as night skies or interior shots.

Contain yourself

Video is stored within what's called a container file – commonly AVI (audio video interleave) – which stores the compressed video and audio data together. Containers can actually hold video compressed with different codecs, so you could have one AVI with DivX encoded video and

another with MPEG-2, although not at the same time. Other container formats you'll encounter are QuickTime, WMV and MKV, to name a few.

In order to play back video, you first need a program that can handle the container – such as Windows Media Player for AVI, or Apple's QuickTime Player for QuickTime – and then you need the necessary codec installed to decode the file. Some players, such as Window Media Player, will attempt to locate and download a codec for you, but not all. If it fails, you'll need to manually download and install it, which is a relatively pain-free procedure that typically involves nothing more than downloading a file and following a wizard to install it – just make sure you have a virus checker to check the download, just in case.

MPEG-2

MPEG-2 is used to encode DVD movies and was developed by the Moving Picture Expert Group as a replacement for MPEG-1, which was used with the little-known VideoCD format. It can be used for high-definition material, but it creates large file sizes compared to more recent codecs that have been designed specifically with HD material in mind. Use of the MPEG-2 codec requires a fee to be paid, and there isn't a free version available for download legally.

MPEG-4

MPEG-4 was introduced by the Moving Picture Expert Group as its next-generation codec to replace MPEG-2 (MPEG-3 was in development for a short time, but was abandoned as it could easily be confused with MP3 audio compression). MPEG-4 is actually a collection of standards, referred to as parts, which ensures compatibility between different encoders and players that support a specific part. The main

The most common video codecs you'll see in action.

Since each 1080p frame equates to a 1920 x 1080 image, one uncompressed frame is a huge 6MB file.

"Compression is employed to reduce the volume of data to a more manageable amount"

parts you're likely to encounter currently are MPEG4 part 2, which is used in codecs such as DivX, XviD and QuickTime 6, and MPEG-4 part 10, which is used by H.264, QuickTime 7 and Blu-ray.

DivX
DivX originally started life as a hack of Microsoft's MPEG-4 codec to make it work with a wider range of container formats. However, version 4 was a complete rewrite from scratch, making it a legitimate codec. The codec was widely used in the early days of DVD ripping to compress movies so they could be fitted on a CD. If you just want to play back DivX video files, the codec is available to download from *www.divx.com*. If you want to create your own DivX videos, there's a range of tools available, some free and others that you have to pay for.

XviD
During the early development of DivX, the first legitimate version was released under an open-source licence, which allows other people to access the source code and even adapt or change it. Many products, such as the Linux operating system or the OpenOffice.org office suite, are released under open-source licences. XviD is an open-source version of the DivX codec based on the initial first release, but since developed separately. The codec is freely available from *www.xvid.org*.

WMV HD
WMV HD is Microsoft's offering to the HD encoding world, based – as you may have guessed – on its WMV format. WMV HD uses the existing DVD disc to store movies, but uses the WMV codec to compress the video sufficiently to allow an HD version of a movie to be squeezed into the same space that an SD DVD version would occupy.

WMV HD discs were occasionally used for special edition DVD releases before Blu-ray was widely available, but it's rarely used now. The codec can still be used for online HD video though, and is also supported by Microsoft's Xbox 360 games console.

MPEG-4 H.264 / AVC
Also known as AVC (Advanced Video Coding), H.264 / AVC is the MPEG-4 part 10 standard. It was originally started with the aim of creating a codec that could compress video to comparable visual quality as MPEG-2, but in half as much space or less. Like MPEG-2, it requires the payment of a fee to use the codec. It's occasionally encountered in high-definition video downloads, but more commonly used to encode video Blu-ray discs, and is also used by the BBC for its HD broadcasts on satellite

VC-1
VC-1 is an evolution of the WMV codec originally developed by Microsoft, and is the most common alternative to H.264 / AVC. Significantly, it's supported by Blu-ray discs as a mandatory codec that all players must be able to decode and is also Microsoft's preferred codec for the Xbox 360 games console. Like H.264 / AVC, it requires a licence fee to implement, although it can also be found bundled for free with many Microsoft products. *ⓖ*

Optical discs make use of codecs, too – otherwise, a Blu-ray movie wouldn't last five minutes.

Most codecs can be found on the internet and will install with little fuss.

97

Enjoying cutting-edge content is about more than just that big screen in the corner. The options for turning your front room into a home cinema are almost endless, and it needn't be hugely complicated or expensive, either. Whether you want a recorder for your digital TV, an amp and speakers to beef up your audio system – or an HD projector to get that true big-screen experience – we'll look at the right option for you.

Introducing home cinema

An HDTV is only the starting point of a home cinema experience. To get the most out of your new TV, you'll also need a surround-sound system

When it comes to getting the best from your HDTV, there are a bewildering number of options available in both the video and audio spheres. With careful choices, you can build a system that will grow with you, giving you a far more immersive and dramatic experience.

One of the first additions most people will want to make to their new TV is a way of recording broadcasts. And, while Freeview isn't available yet in HD, it's nonetheless one of the richest sources of content. Whether you choose to use old-fashioned DVDs or integrated set-top boxes with multiple tuners and hard disks is up to you. We cover your options over the page.

Beyond that, there are multiple levels you can reach to get the entertainment system you're after, from an enhanced audio system through to – quite literally – a home cinema, with a projector and more speakers than you can shake a stick at. We'll cover all the options in this chapter.

All-in-ones
All-in-one systems (*see p110*) are the simplest and cheapest way to get that home-cinema experience. For one low price, you'll get an amplifier and speakers, and possibly a DVD player, too. Most come with five speakers and a subwoofer, and are capable of decoding Dolby Digital and DTS audio soundtracks. The principle advantage is that all the cabling and other bits you need are included, and the speakers will be specifically matched to the amp.

Alternatively, you can buy a pseudo-surround system, either as separate speakers or an integrated unit known as a soundbar (*see p109*). The latter can be mounted under (or over) a wall-mounted TV for the neatest approach. The results from both systems can be astounding, although it's difficult to beat having speakers mounted behind you.

Separate lives
For the best setup possible, though, you'll need to invest in 'separates' (*see p105 onwards*). These can cost anything from a few hundred pounds for everything, up to thousands of pounds per component. It's really a matter of what you're willing to spend and, while there's a steep law of diminishing returns, you do generally get what you pay for.

What's important, though, is balance – there's no point

blitzing £2000 on an amp unless you plan to splash out on a commensurately glamorous pair of speakers to match it. Similarly, expensive may not mean good value if you're not going to use all the features, particularly in the case of complex kit such as AV amplifiers. Our advice is to decide on your budget and then split it equally between all the separate components, with 5-10% budgeted for accessories. While we do draw the line at paying £200 for a single cable, take a look at p112 for why you shouldn't skimp on the extras.

Starter's orders
At its most basic, a dedicated amp and speakers will beef up those that came attached to your TV. As we see on p106 and p109, this needn't cost a fortune, and you'll be left with a much more satisfying movie and music experience.

The next step up from that is an AV amplifier. This has inputs for all of your devices, including a games console, DVD player and satellite box, as well as outputs for audio and video. The AV amplifier then plugs into your TV, so you choose what to watch and listen to on the AV amplifier rather than juggling several remotes.

More than this, the AV amplifier also decodes sound and pipes it out to the speakers. You should look for one that supports HDMI inputs. Even the cheapest will support Dolby Digital and DTS sound decoding, but the more expensive models will support the new HD standards including Dolby Digital EX and DTS-ES, which produce better sound – we'll cover all you need to know on these, too, on p114.

The big-screen experience
Unless you've spent the turnover of a small European nation on your screen, it's still unlikely to be big enough to accommodate an epic film in its full glory. And, sometimes, only scale will do. This is where projectors come in, offering the perfect complement to your everyday system.

While they're a relatively cheap way of getting a big screen when needed, again, make sure you get the features you need, particularly if you have a difficult space to project in. You should also factor in the price of replacement bulbs – which can be alarmingly expensive – and, ideally, a projector screen to get the best from you HD home cinema (*see p116 for more*). ●

"There are a bewildering number of options available in both the video and audio spheres"

Introducing PVRs

The VCR is dead, in its place we have the PVR, adding myriad new features along the way. We hack a way through the jungle of options

Having two Freeview tuners on board will give you added flexibility to watch one channel while another is recording, or record both at once.

Check the back of any PVR you buy for component or HDMI outputs to get the best quality.

A combo PVR combines the best of both worlds, with a hard disk for recording and a DVD burner for archival.

Features such as a series link or an EPG make both choosing and recording TV programmes an absolute doddle.

When the video recorder came along in the 1980s, it changed the way we watched TV. No longer were we tied to the TV schedules; we could simply stick a tape in, set a time and channel, and watch at our leisure. Assuming we'd programmed everything correctly, of course.

Then, DVD recorders took over, offering more convenience, greater quality and easier storage than was possible before. And, more recently, hard disk recording has been pioneered by TiVo in the US, then popularised by Sky+ in the UK, and followed by a whole rash of Freeview PVRs (personal video recorders).

Digital TV has also brought the convenience of the EPG to modern recorders, letting you record entire series (also called series link) without the need to enter start times, end times or 53-digit codes. Press a button and it's all done for you – and all without the need to find a child to program it.

DVD recorders

If you plan to keep your recordings for a while, your best bet is a player with a built-in DVD recorder, as recordings can then be filed away somewhere safe. But not all recorders are equal and, for the purposes of recording TV, many don't have digital tuners or EPGs built in. Also, you're ultimately limited in terms of recording time, and the only way to fit more on the disc is to reduce the quality.

You should also check the recorder's ability to play back commercial DVDs, since many come equipped with decent upscaling features capable of breathing new HD life into your existing movie collection. Finally, check on format support for recording: most, but not all, will support all the variants of recordable DVD format – write-once DVD+R and DVD-R, plus recordable DVD+RW, DVD-RW and DVD-RAM.

Hard disk recorders

Hard disk recorders are more convenient than DVD-based PVRs, as you don't need to keep swapping out individual discs. But you'll still run out of space eventually if you hoard dozens of movies, even with larger-capacity recorders.

All hard disk recorders allow you to pause, rewind and then catch back up with live TV, but, again, they're not all equal. Not all have twin tuners, for example, which allow you to record one programme while watching another or, if your TV also has a digital tuner, watch one programme while recording two others.

Also check whether your intended PVR has series link – not all do – and how far in advance the EPG goes. If you're going away on holiday for two weeks and want to record a programme in the second week, an eight-day guide isn't going to cut it. If at all possible, see a demo of the guide – a well laid-out, speedy version can make a big difference down the line.

Remember that you won't get HD broadcasts with these boxes for the time being, though – you'll need a Sky HD or Virgin V+ set-top box for that, which also come with subscription costs – take a look at p78 for more on these.

Best of both worlds

Thankfully, you can also get combination PVRs with both hard disk and DVD drive to play back and record discs, though you'll pay more for the privilege. That means you can replace your DVD player, recorder and Freeview devices with just one box (and one remote control), enjoy the convenience of recording to hard disk with pause, rewind and catch-up of live TV, and then have the option to archive any recordings to disc when you need to free up space on the drive. ⓖ

HDD PVRs

➔ LG 42LT75

Price:	£820
Internet:	www.lge.co.uk
Rating:	★★★★☆

Don't want an extra box lying around your living space? Well, here's a 42in TV that has a fully functioning Freeview+ PVR tucked inside its svelte LCD chassis. Its 160GB HDD offers such recording finery as series link, joining together shows interrupted by, say, a news broadcast, and adjusting the start and end times to account for late listings changes. The remote control and menus switch between PVR and TV functions brilliantly, and the TV itself is HD Ready, and comes with a high claimed contrast ratio of 8000:1.

The only disappointment is that you can't record more than one digital stream simultaneously, but recordings from the digital tuner are absolutely immaculate, and analogue channels decent enough too. It's not the finest screen around, but its never less than watchable and, given the features and price – plus the convenience – it an option that will surely find many fans.

➔ TOPFIELD TF5810PVR

Price:	£300
Internet:	www.topfield.co.uk
Rating:	★★★★★

Everything about this unit is serious. It's not just well-built but also strikingly chic and scores a coup over cheapo rivals by sporting an HDMI output through which it can squirt Freeview broadcasts and recordings upscaled to 1080i HD. There's a USB port that lets you transfer files to and from a PC, plus support for MP3 (JPEG, GIF and bitmap images can be supported via an update), so we're glad of the 500GB of storage: enough for 250 hours of TV programmes.

You can edit out sections of a recording – goodbye, Mr Advert – and twin tuners mean you can record two digital programmes while watching a another, or watch two live shows via the Picture in Picture function. The only bum note is the cluttered remote control. You'll get superbly crisp recordings too, although some glitches creep in where programmes are edited. Nothing though, stops this from being the most seriously impressive Freeview PVR to date.

➔ HUMAX PVR-9200T

Price:	£150
Internet:	www.humaxdigital.co.uk
Rating:	★★★★★

It's been around for a while, but this is still one of our firm favourites. You can fit in up to 70 hours of recordings via the two Freeview tuners and there's a picture in picture facility so you can watch two different programmes at the same time too. And there's even a modicum of editing flexibility as the unit lets you cut out bits of recordings you don't want. The menu, and the Electronic Programme Guide in particular, are all but numpty-proof.

The only negative thing we can say about the 9200T at this point really, is that it lacks an HDMI connection for all-digital hook up, and won't do any upscaling of your recordings or Freeview broadcasts. But it has precious little impact on the outstanding recordings, with rich detail and colours. This was an instant classic when it first came out, and aside from the lack of upscaling or HDMI, age hasn't diminished it. In fact, its plummeting price has arguably made it better – you should find it online for a bargain price.

➔ GOODMANS GHD8020F2

Price:	£65
Internet:	www.amazon.co.uk
Rating:	★★★★★

Beyond the unpromising wedge of greyish plastic, there lies gold. Getting the worst out of the way, there's no HDMI output to output upscaled footage – hardly surprising at this price, and there's only a modest 80GB of storage. But it starts looking up with the well organised and presented operating system, with five provided favourite channel lists and a superb electronic programme guide. Two digital tuners allows you to record two different Freeview channels at once, or watch one channel while you record another. Even better, the unit continually caches the channel it's tuned to, so if you miss the start of a programme, you can just rewind back to the start. As for storage, it's still enough to hold up to 35 hours, and recordings are remarkably good too – far better than you've any right to expect for the price. You'll naturally get more features, more memory and even better performance if you're willing to pay more for them, but this is one of the best PVR bargains we've seen.

➔ PANASONIC DMR-EX88

Price:	£390
Internet:	www.panasonic.co.uk
Rating:	★★★★★

Not only does this combi recorder look all slinky and high-tech, it's impressively robust and comes with a truly prodigious specification. Alongside the DVD recorder sits a ruddy great 400GB hard disk, able to store up to 712 hours of TV, as well as music ripped from CDs and multimedia files dumped onto via the SD card or USB inputs. Also significant is the Freeview+ badge, which means it has Series Link and can automatically join programmes interrupted by news broadcasts. Flexibility is the keyword, with four recording quality options, plus the ability to delete sections, insert chapter breaks or even re-edit chapters into a totally different order. You can also copy edited HDD recordings to DVD at up to 75x real time, and create menus for them. But despite the sophistication, it's remarkably easy to use, and picture quality is brilliant too. DVD playback is immaculate too, with a tasty onboard 1080p upscaling system. We're not going to pretend it's cheap, but if you want an all-singing, all-dancing recorder, this is it.

➔ SONY RDR-HXD890

Price:	£220
Internet:	www.sony.co.uk
Rating:	★★★★☆

By sub-£250 standards, there's plenty to like here. There's a 160GB hard disk (capable of storing up to 455 hours of TV), as well as a very capable DVD recording section capable of burning to all the major disc types, and playing DVD-RAM discs too. It can play MP3, JPEG and DivX files from discs or USB storage devices, as well as working as a digital photo album or music jukebox. You can even dump your HDD camcorder movies onto it. There's an HDMI socket through which it can upscale standard definition sources to 1080p, and the resulting performance is highly impressive.

Pictures from its digital tuner are among the best we've seen, and it also succeeds superbly as a DVD player, with the upscaler adding detail in good-looking droves. Our only disappointment is the one digital and one analogue tuner (rather than two digital ones), meaning you can't watch one Freeview-only channel while recording another. But it's not enough to stop us loving the gorgeous AV quality and performance – helped by one of the nicest operating systems around.

➔ TOSHIBA RD-98DT

Price:	£240
Internet:	www.toshiba.co.uk
Rating:	★★★★☆

There are lots of goodies inside this ultra-streamlined box. The 250GB HDD at its heart is a very sensible capacity, but the real attraction is the versatile DVD recorder sitting alongside it. It can record to most disc formats for archival, including 8GB dual-layer DVD-R discs, and can also handle MP3 and DivX files. Ordinary DVDs look great, and there's both a v1.3 HDMI output and a 1080p upscaler to to give DVDs an extra 'kind of high def' sparkle, which works superbly. The resulting pictures look more detailed and sharp-edged without adding noise – and that's as much as you could fairly ask at this price.

Three different recording modes, are available, giving great results in all but the lowest quality option, which is best avoided. In an ideal world, the pictures from the tuner would be a touch richer, and the remote control more intuitive. But by real world standards, this is top choice for those looking for a broadcast box that will also lavish some attention on your collection of nice shiny discs.

➔ TVONICS DTR-Z250

Price:	£200
Internet:	www.tvonics.com
Rating:	★★★★☆

Easily the most visually eye-catching Freeview PVR to hit the high street, its cutely rounded corners, glossy finish and ability to work vertically or horizontally set it apart. Inside, you'll find a healthy 250GB hard drive (a 500GB version is also available), holding as much as 125 hours of video recordings. As with most models on the market, there are twin digital tuners on-board so you can record two Freeview broadcasts at the same time, or record one while watching another. It meets the official 'Freeview+' standard too, and so supports such treats as one-button Series Link and automatic timer adjustment in the event of delays.

Helping you round is an unusually neat operating system and Electronic Programme Guide, making it child's play to use. Performance is a winner too – and that's despite the otherwise slightly disappointing lack of an HDMI output or video upscaling facility. We can't help lamenting the lack of any editing options either. But with so much style and talent for the features it does have, this is a great choice at a reasonably affordable price.

Introducing amps and AV receivers

Now you've got the picture sorted, it's time to give your audio system a boost...

Check which digital formats your receiver supports – not all will cope with HD audio.

With inputs and outputs all in one place, a receiver can bring tremendous flexibility to your setup.

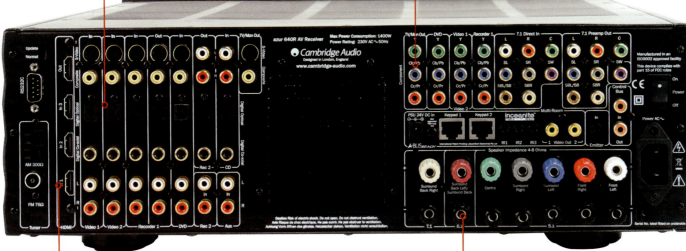

With multiple HDMI inputs, this model can also act as a signal splitter.

An AV receiver acts as the central point to get your speakers working with all your other AV equipment.

In order to get signals to the right level to feed speakers, you'll need to amplify them. You have a couple of options here – for just a pair of stereo speakers, you can either buy a pair of active speakers (with an amp built in) or passive speakers and a stereo amplifier.

Stereo amplifiers

In this case, you're taking just the analogue or digital stereo output from your HD source (or sources) and feeding them direct to a pair of speakers (and possibly a third, dedicated bass speaker – a subwoofer). Normally, an amp will have a couple of inputs that can either be switched on the unit itself, or via a remote control.

How much you spend is dependent on the features you need, although higher prices will generally give you better sound – when partnered with the right speakers, that is. In this case, that would mean dealing with music sources and film soundtracks with equal finesse. But the golden rule of buying AV kit applies here, too – try to split your spend equally between the speakers and the amp, with ample budget left for cabling. We have our pick of the market for you on p105.

AV receivers

If your ambitions are on a slightly grander scale, such as surround sound (or you have multiple sources you want to control), you're better served by an AV receiver. This will take all your audio sources (and often video ones, too), decode the multichannel audio and feed it to your speakers and TV using minimum wiring. You'll also get individual control of each speaker, so you can tweak the overall balance to perfection.

Not all current models will deal with every one of the new HD and surround formats (see p114), so study the plethora of badges on the front of the unit to see what you're actually getting – some of these labels are more important than others. Also, look out for features such as auto-calibration, which will set up your speakers for you; HDMI video switching, to make up for a shortfall of future-proofed sockets on the TV itself; and the useful ability to upscale SD sources.

Do your homework

Before settling on either, carefully consider what your requirements are now, as well as in the future. Be realistic about what features you really need to shell out for – do you really need support for all the 7.1 formats?

Consider the size of room you're buying for, too: power figures are quoted in Watts and, as a general rule, 20W per channel will be plenty for most purposes. This figure can be measured in many ways by manufacturers, so make sure components are measured from 20Hz to 20KHz (the range of human hearing) at 8 Ohms and 0.08% distortion or similar. That will provide a good indication of the real-world measurement of the kit you're buying. ⓘ

> An AV receiver will provide for practically any AV setup. Alternatively, an integrated amplifier will provide a simpler option.

Amplifiers

These stereo amplifiers might not stretch to surround-sound setups but they could transform the sound coming out of your speakers

➔ CAMBRIDGE AUDIO AZUR 340A SE

Price	£180
Internet	www.cambridgeaudio.com
Rating	★★★★★

If you're looking for a basic stereo amp to give your HDTV's audio a boost, look no further than this bargain of a box. It covers all the bases perfectly, with the very model of a well-designed front panel, easy-to-use remote and a good, solid sound. There are six sets of stereo analogue RCA inputs at the rear, plus a mini-jack on the front for hooking up your MP3 player (the remote can also control iPods) – there are no digital inputs.

But analogue doesn't stop the 340A SE from sounding fantastic, with well-controlled and punchy reproductions of movie soundtracks, and an equally skilful handling of music. With 45W per channel, you have plenty of choice for speakers – we'd put this amp with a reasonably neutral-sounding pair to compensate for its slight over-enthusiasm in the top end. You can also take advantage of the dual speaker-binding posts for bi-wiring, leading to a much improved sound.

➔ ROTEL RA-04

Price	£250
Internet	www.rotel.com/uk
Rating	★★★★★

If you're happy to splash out a little more than £180, this slim unit from Rotel rewards with a few more features than the Cambridge Audio. There's still the MP3 player input (albeit without the iPod control), but you'll also get speaker switching between the two separate speaker outputs – handy for using one pair for movies and one for music.

There's no remote supplied, but that, conversely, can be seen as a bonus – less circuitry means a cleaner sound in the world of amplifiers, and the RA-04 certainly delivers here. It's well behaved over a wide range of material, although some amps will bring a larger-than-life sound to more violent movie soundtracks. Note that at 40W per channel it will struggle with larger rooms. But its talent over all types of material makes this a great first addition to an HDTV setup – it could easily last you for years as a dedicated music amp if you decide to upgrade to surround sound later.

➔ NAD C352

Price	£300
Internet	http://nadelectronics.com
Rating	★★★★☆

Stretch your budget to £300 and your range of choice reaches the bottom end of NAD's legendary range of amplifiers. Packing in 80W per channel, there's enough power to comfortably handle a huge range of speakers.

That power also extends to give a good dynamic treatment to almost any material you throw at it, with the precision handling of mid-range tones a particular highlight. That has good implications for movie soundtracks in general, and the clarity of dialogue in particular. Music is also handled skilfully, with the ability to convey a very deep sound stage and separate individual instruments with ease. As with all of the amps on this page, its flexibility at handling differing types of material is what makes it worthy of consideration, and its strength is its brand name and that 80W of power. Only the less than industrial build quality lets it down.

➔ ROKSAN KANDY K2

Price	£750
Internet	www.roksan.co.uk
Rating	★★★★★

From one of the sturdiest names we know comes this brave-looking new amp. The Roksan Kandy K2 should definitely be on your shortlist if you're planning a larger system, or are fussy about your sound.

It excels at rendering complex material (including soundtracks), managing to keep individual details distinct without affecting the overall unity of a soundtrack: it's bounding with energy and punch when fed upbeat music, but can also deal with the subtleties of a brooding movie atmosphere. Such even-temperedness means that choosing a suitable pair of speakers is made much easier, and the 125W per channel provides as much heft as most rooms will stand. We're not going to pretend that either the unit or its otherwise decent remote are going to match any of your other separates, but when they sound this good, we can learn to forgive it.

AV receivers

For the more complex setup, a good AV receiver will simplify things enormously – here are some of the best

➲ ONKYO TX-NR905

Price:	£1400
Internet:	www.onkyo.co.uk
Rating:	★★★★★

Towering high and looking completely indomitable, this is 24kg of unapologetic AV beefcake, and we love it. As you'd hope of an AV receiver costing this much, it's also overloaded to bursting point with connections and features. These include four HDMI inputs, two HDMI outputs (with outstanding 1080p upscaling in between); a humungous power rating of 7 x 220W; full Dolby TrueHD, DTS HD and DTS Master Audio decoding; THX Select 2 certification; three-zone multiroom support; and full network integration – including internet radio – via an Ethernet input.

But its the performance that really makes us giddy. Its astonishing raw power, together with the quality of its innards enable it to produce quality across the board seldom witnessed for under two grand. Given that this is one of the best AV receivers we've ever come across, it's even more tantalising that you should be able to find it for rather less than this price if you take a scout round online.

➲ PIONEER VSX-1018

Price:	£500
Internet:	www.pioneer.co.uk
Rating:	★★★★★

If you like bang for buck, this will have you drooling. Go for the black model and it'll scream 'take me seriously' at the top of its 7 x 150W lungs. Its bounty of features starts with support for all the new big HD audio formats: Dolby TrueHD, DTS-HD Master Audio and DTS-HD High Resolution. There are 7.1 audio line inputs if you'd rather have a Blu-ray player do the decoding, built-in iPod and USB ports, and a built-in WMA9 Pro decoder to play digital audio from a PC. It's even earned the 'THX Select 2 Plus' seal of approval from George Lucas's LucasFilm.

Thankfully the quality is abundantly obvious with or without a George Lucas level of home cinema, with everything we'd ask for at this price and more. The sole disappointment is the two HDMI inputs when we'd expect at least three. But this isn't enough to stop this £500 AV receiver that looks and sounds like a £700 one. And you can't really ask for much more than that.

➲ DENON AVR-1909

Price:	£450
Internet:	www.denon.co.uk
Rating:	★★★★★

This surprisingly affordable model from home cinema legend Denon delivers the key Dolby TrueHD and DTS-Master Audio decoding support, while providing three HDMI inputs, an HDMI output and built-in 1080p video upscaling. It pumps out 7 x 90W channels of audio power and uses a very effective, microphone-based, semi-automatic set-up system. On the downside, there's no ethernet or USB input support – iPods can be accommodated via an optional dock – and there's no THX accreditation.

But any sound quality concerns from that were destroyed in emphatic fashion with everything we cared to throw at it. With an uncanny sense of when to be aggressive and when to be understated while watching films, it never sounds anything less than completely precise and immersive across the board. It also delivers the goods with its video upscaling, producing cleaner, sharper results than any other receivers we've seen below £500. If you've got a number of HD sources, it's an excellent option.

➲ SONY STR-DG820

Price:	£300
Internet:	www.sony.co.uk
Rating:	★★★★★

This may look like a budget option, but don't be fooled. The biggest single surprise is its ability to decode Dolby TrueHD and DTS-HD Master Audio sound formats, and deliver them over 7.1 channels. It's also built like the proverbial, cutting down vibrations, while its innards keep audio and video signals running short distances to reduce interference – the sort of stuff usually saved for high-end receivers.

Four HDMI inputs is impressive, but video upscaling and 7.1 analogue audio inputs are absent, saved for the models higher in Sony's range. These minor negatives aren't hard to bear at this price, though – especially once it becomes clear just what a startlingly good performer it is. With a surprising amount of power (7 x 100W) to play with, it mines movie soundtracks for every last tinkle of detail and rumble of bass, as well as handling music delicately or assertively where necessary. All told, it's left looking like one of the very best options at this price.

Introducing speakers

For great film soundtracks and music you'll need more than your TV's speakers

Tweeters and squawkers Not all speakers will come with these specialised speaker drivers, but those that do will have much better mid- and top-end performance.

Woofer This is where most of the body of the sound comes from, with the most basic speakers comprising just a single one of these.

Port This particular speaker has a front port for defining the bass end of the sound, but many speakers are rear-ported and need a little room at the back to sound their best.

C hoosing a suitable speaker setup is trickier than you'd think. You've got options all the way from tiny stereo speakers to monstrous 7.1 setups, the latter of which will quickly fill your lounge with boxes and wires. But with so much focus on picture quality, don't forget about the audio side of the equation.

There are two main types of speaker: bookshelf units and floorstanders. As a general rule, floorstanders will produce the better sound, as they're larger and have more room for drivers. Bookshelf speakers can simply be put either side of your TV or, even better, on stands or wall mounted. They both come in a range of different sizes and shapes – which you go for depends largely on the budget and space you have to work with.

Woofers and tweeters
Inside a speaker, you'll find a number of cones, called drivers. These come in three different types: woofers, which produce low-frequency bass; tweeters, which produce high-frequency treble; and mid-range (also called squawkers), which fill in the space in-between. The number of drivers in a speaker can be determined by the naming 'x-way'.

For example, a three-way speaker has three drivers. An entry-level two-way speaker will have one tweeter and one woofer; higher-end speakers introduce more woofers, tweeters and mid-range drivers to increase sound quality by giving each frequency range its own specialised and tuned driver, leading to a more precise sound.

When you buy speakers, you'll find they have two main specifications: power, measured in Watts, and impedance, measured in Ohms. It's a good idea to make sure your speakers match up with your amplifier's Wattage and impedance ratings, particularly as you get into higher-end kit. You'll be able to find this information in your amplifier's manual, or check the manufacturers website.

For getting the very deepest bass (great for film soundtracks), you'll also need a specialised speaker – called a subwoofer – which can deal with the lowest gut-worrying rumbles. If your speakers don't come with one, you'll again need to match it to your other speakers and your amplifier (although some TVs also have a subwoofer output). The idea is to get a subwoofer with a frequency response that overlaps that of your other speakers. You'll find some speaker suggestions opposite.

Stereo and 5.1 speakers

You don't need to spend thousands on speakers – here's our selection of flexible options

➲ CAMBRIDGE AUDIO S30

Price	£120
Internet	www.cambridgeaudio.com
Rating	★★★★★

If space is limited, or you just want to add welly to your TV's speakers, these great-value bookshelf speakers will do the job nicely. Not only are they smart to look at, but they sound rather marvellous, too. They'll handle film dialogue and atmospheric soundtracks with equal panache, and sound effects are delivered with requisite crispness and clarity. Rumbling bass is beyond their remit, but as long as you're careful with placing (away from the wall and, ideally, on stands) they'll manage a surprising amount of heft.

As a front end for your entertainment system, these speakers are also very capable of handling music, with a tightness and range that makes attaching them to an amp and CD player a pleasing prospect.

➲ ONKYO HTX-22D

Price	£300
Internet	www.eu.onkyo.com
Rating	★★★★☆

Sick of weedy sound dribbling from your HDTV's speakers? Plug your AV kit into one end of this, and the other into your TV via HDMI. You can then easily switch between all your devices and change their volume using the one well laid-out remote. Setup and expandability are impressive, with support for cutting-edge HD audio formats and the ability to add extra speakers (up to 5.1 surround sound).

The result is a neat and compact system that'll give masses more scale, range and impact than even the best built-in TV set – especially if you use the DTS Surround Sensation feature. Its size and price mean it's not the last word in home cinema or sheer quality, but it's a great start.

➲ MONITOR AUDIO BRONZE BR5

Price	£400
Internet	monitoraudio.co.uk
Rating	★★★★★

You can pay much more for a pair of floorstander speakers than this, but when they sound and look this good we'd advise taking a listen to the BR5s first. Paired with even a low-powered amp, these boxes will deliver superb clarity.

They're less shy and retiring when it comes to appearance, with their floor spikes, sharp lines and a distinct bulk, but that gives them plenty of authority. The top end of the bass is well controlled, there's a pleasing airiness to the treble, too. There's not quite as much movement as we'd like when it comes to bone-shaking film soundtracks, it's impressively balanced and in control.

It all results in an attractively neutral tone, just as at home with jangly guitars as majestic soundtracks. If you've got the space, they're both flexible and good-value.

➲ KEF KHT1005.2

Price	£400
Internet	www.kef.co.uk
Rating	★★★★★

These quirky-looking egg-shaped units are a fantastic way to get started with a 5.1 system. Considering the top-drawer performance, they're a bit of a bargain. The satellite speakers are diminutive, but they still pack in two-way drivers – sort of. The 14mm tweeter actually sits in the middle of a larger, 7.5cm driver that handles the mid-range. Backing all that up is a 100W active subwoofer, with its downward-facing 20cm port pumping out a convincingly rumbling bass.

The combination of a clean and sweet top-end, well-controlled and crunchy mid-range, plus a surprisingly authoritative low-end makes the KHT1005s an absolute steal at this price. If your living room is on the palatial side, they'll struggle to retain their power, but that's the only potential downside.

Home cinema all-in-one systems

For sheer convenience, it's hard to beat an all-in-one home cinema system, with integrated disc players, amps and speakers...

➲ PIONEER LX01

Price:	**£1450**
Internet:	**www.pioneer.co.uk**
Rating:	★★★★★

It's expensive, yes, but take a closer look at this DVD-based system and you'll start to see why. Firstly, it looks stunning; the main speakers are unfeasibly small and cheekily sculpted, while the remote is positively iconic. There's Freeview recording to DVD or a 250GB HDD, it can also store media files and rip CDs (making it a decent media jukebox) and it'll upscale DVDs to 1080p. There are three HDMI inputs and one output, and it'll support HD audio from external Blu-ray decks. The satellite speakers are omnidirectional, giving majestic surround sound performance, the scale and precision of which puts much larger designs to shame. Picture quality is extremely good, so if your after supreme design and performance standards, this is an outstanding surround sound proposition.

➲ PANASONIC SC-BT100

Price:	**From £700**
Internet:	**www.panasonic.co.uk**
Rating:	★★★★★

DVDs, frankly, just aren't HD enough. So hooray for this system, with a Blu-ray player built in. It comes in three configurations: a 3.1 system for £700; 5.1 for £850; and 7.1 for £1000, which comes with two pairs of wireless rear speakers. It's Blu-ray Profile 1.1 compatible, so will do picture-in-picture, handle some HD audio soundtracks, and HD JPEG photos via its SD card slot – but there's no internet-based BD-Live available. The extra detail Blu-ray delivers gives pictures that no DVD-based system can compete with. The upscaling algorithms are among the best we've seen too. The sound isn't as accomplished as its ground-breaking HD pictures: the slightly ugly speakers are solid in the bass and mid areas, but a touch harsh in the treble area. But then you can't have everything. And just being able to enjoy HD pictures and audio so easily makes it a tantalising option.

➲ LG HT953TV

Price:	**£580**
Internet:	**www.lge.co.uk**
Rating:	★★★★★

With each speaker over a metre tall and a stand-mounted DVD deck, this isn't a subtle option... and then there's the voluminous subwoofer. But it sure is pretty. The floorstanding speakers taper in at the bottom delightfully, and the pole-mounted DVD deck looks like something out of *Star Trek*. Feature highlights include 1080p DVD upscaling, an iPod iDock, DiVX support, sonic tuning by Mark Levinson, the ability to rip CDs to USB memory sticks or MP3 players. It also has 10.1-channel playback that creates five extra 'virtual' speakers alongside the real ones. We were initially cynical, but it's surprisingly effective, if a touch muddy. The results are excellent for such a reasonably priced package. Mid-range is clear and natural, treble never harsh and the sub delivers lovely dollops of bass. With perfectly crisp, noiseless pictures those with the room (a room 20m² or more) should consider this as the best mid-price all-in-one system in town.

Speaker setup

Correct placement of speakers is crucial for getting the best sound, and the same rules apply regardless of the environment

Ideal setup

In an perfect world, the primary viewing seat would sit in the centre or slightly forward of the back of the room. Rear speakers should be placed behind or to either side of the seating, and pointing at the listener, using stands or wall mounting as necessary. Doing that will ensure you get the best tone and balance from the rear speakers, which are often limited in their frequency response. You'd then have the front stereo pair either side of the display, with a centre speaker directly below or above the screen.

While upper and mid frequencies are highly directional – that is, you can pinpoint where they're coming from with some accuracy – that isn't the case with lower bass frequencies. As such, you can put a subwoofer almost anywhere in the room and it will still have the same stomach-rumbling potential. The side or rear are both fine, as long as it's away from sources of rattling.

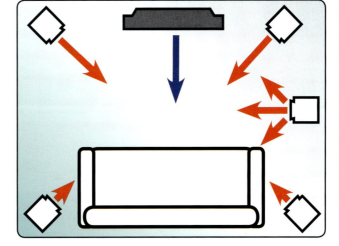

STANDS

Even in the perfect environment, don't neglect your speaker stands, as a solid footing will keep the sound focused and stable. Pay a little attention to your speaker cables, too, and you'll be richly rewarded. See over the page for more.

Corner setup

A favourite spot for hefty old CRTs was in the corner, with everything else arranged around it. That's fine if you're just replacing it with a flat-panel TV, but far from ideal if you're also adding surround (or even stereo) speakers. Unless you've got a very small seating area, you'll find it tricky to get a large enough 'sweet spot', where the sound is perfectly balanced.

If rearranging the room isn't an option, it's no big disaster – you'll just have to experiment a little to get the best possible sound from your new setup. The biggest problem you're likely to face is getting the speakers balanced across all your seating, so you may have to focus on one or two seating positions.

The other issue is that of furniture getting in the way, as this can unduly affect what you're hearing, whether by directly blocking the sound or by area reflections causing a delay that will muddy the sound. You can avoid this problem by placing everything as symmetrically as possible and tweaking the position of the speakers until they sound their best. Auto setup routines on AV receivers will also help you out here.

L-shaped setup

Assuming you don't live in an aircraft hangar or a grain silo, an L-shaped setup is about the trickiest home cinema environment you're likely to face. The void part of the room will begin swallowing bass frequencies coming from the subwoofer so, depending on how much of the lower end this is responsible for, it can sap the life out of your carefully chosen setup.

If you know your home cinema setup is going to be set up in this type of room, try going for something that spreads the frequencies out a little more to larger satellite speakers – that will keep some of the lower end coming from all directions.

Otherwise, the best advice is to keep the front stereo pair as focused on the seating area as possible in order to keep the stereo image stable. Again, experiment by moving furniture around and placing the speakers in different positions and heights until you're happy.

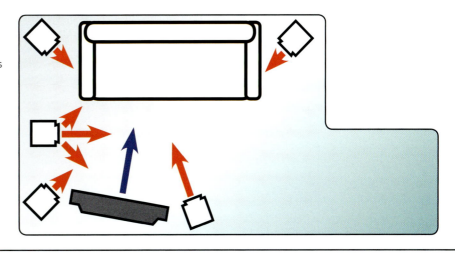

Improving your system

Don't let your system suffer through poor setup – cables, supports and mains filtering can make a difference

By now, if you've been paying attention, you'll have spent a decent wedge of cash on a high-definition TV, recording device, speakers and possibly a surround-sound receiver and amp.

So far so good, but the spending isn't over yet. While there's nothing criminal about simply sticking your TV on a cheap unit from Ikea and hooking it all up with the cheapest cables you can find, you won't be getting the most out of your system if you do.

Supports

Your first decision should be what to put your equipment on. Televisions are so heavy these days that just sticking your brand-new 50in plasma on a rickety chipboard unit and hoping for the best won't cut it. Apart from the safety issue, you'll want something stylish to set off all those lovely blue LEDs you so coveted in the shop – and a rack large enough to accommodate all those new bits of kit.

But it isn't just about looks. That wobbly old furniture can transmit vibrations from your new subwoofer to AV equipment – and when that happens, sound quality suffers. Amplifiers are particularly prone to vibrations, as any item of kit that has electrolytic capacitors in sensitive areas of the signal path will be affected.

To keep vibrations to a minimum, look for units with thick, tempered glass shelves and spiked feet, to isolate equipment from vibrations. Atacama's Equinox AV/AV+ models, for example – as well as being multiple award

winners – are superbly built, and there are plenty of optional extras that can be added at a later date, such as cable-management systems, extra shelves and even integrated TV stands.

Left on the shelf

Don't neglect the speaker stand, either. There's no point spending hundreds of pounds on speakers only to tuck them away on a shelf in the corner. Many speakers are rear ported (the hole where the bass comes from) and need space around them to sound their best. And it's even more important to isolate speakers from their surroundings.

Stick them on any old bookshelf and the whole construction will vibrate in sympathy with the speakers and the results will be a jumble. So give your speakers pride of place and plonk them on a sturdy pair of stands. You'll be amazed at the difference a pair of something like Atacama's Nexus 6 stands will make to the way your system sounds: bass becomes more defined, voices project more and music will fill the room in a way it never has before.

The sturdier and heavier your stands are, the less they'll move, and the more your speakers will be able to get on with the job. Most proper speaker stands have a cavity that can be used to add extra weight. Sand will do the job, but for the ultimate mass for volume use Atacama's Atabites (tiny bits of metal) instead. The extra weight damps vibration even more and allows your speakers to shine to their full potential.

Cabling

A lot of people remain unconvinced that spending a lot of money on cables can make a difference to your viewing and listening experience. But, rest assured, if you go for the cheapest you can find or, worse, hook everything up with the cables that come in the box, you'll be missing out on what your system can offer.

There are several factors that affect a cable's ability to do its job. Cables must be shielded properly to reduce interference, resistance must be minimal and they must be resistant to oxidation over time. The plugs at either end also have to be designed to make as snug a contact as possible. Other factors such as capacitance and inductance can also affect the way a cable sounds or performs, and cheaper cables will generally be made from cheaper materials.

Speaker cables

A good place to start is your speaker cables. After all, they're likely to be the longest cables in your system and more prone to interference and signal loss as a result. At the very least, make sure your front pair and centre speakers are hooked up with something decent, as this is where most of the big sound effects originate.

The award-winning QED Silver Anniversary XT cable is a fine budget choice here (£5 per metre). Hook up a set of these and you'll hear more detail, depth and clarity in your movies and music.

If you want to splash out more, feel free, but just be aware that improvements may not be immediately dramatic, or may even change the sound of your system in a way you don't like. Also note that the differences you'll hear will be increasingly subtle the more you spend – good old diminishing returns.

If it's any comfort to your pocket, we're looking at the lower end of the scale here. You could, for instance, plug a set of Nordost's Valhalla cables into your setup, and be rewarded, apparently, with a richer sense of depth, more control over bass and a stunningly transparent and natural sound. The cost? That'll be £2250 for a 0.6m pair.

Video cabling

Depending on the type of connection, varying degrees of improvement can be had with video cables as well. Believe it or not, although the connection is digital, a noticeable difference can often be seen when switching to better-constructed HDMI cables, so don't just go for the cheapest you can lay your hands on.

QED makes a range of mid-priced cables that are excellent value for money. For £50, QED's Qunex HDMI-P cable produces more colourful and punchy pictures than a basic £15 HDMI string, and it holds a connection better, too – it won't fall out if you so much as tweak the position of your TV.

Stands such as this Atacama Equinox AV Plus often come with a huge range of options.

Even replacing cheap mains cables can give your system a boost.

Move up to the £70 Qunex HDMI-SR and you'll see slightly sharper edges, more vibrant colours, less noise and deeper, darker blacks. Next there's the Nordost WyreWizards at £85, or you can spend £250 on Nordost's Silver Screen interconnect. And while there are improvements to be had, you should only spend this sort of money if you're connecting a superb player to a top-of-the-line (not to mention huge) TV.

Scart cables are less of a conundrum. Use a cheap one and your picture quality and sound quality will suffer, big time. The presence of so many thin cables in close proximity can lead to a lot of interference and, as a result, noisy pictures and muddy sound. Good-quality cables aren't expensive – QED's Performance P1210 cable is only £25 – and makes a huge difference to the picture from your Sky+ or Freeview box, with the result being more detail, far less noise and more vibrant colours.

For all non-HDCP video signals, however, such as those between your cable, satellite box, hard disk recorder or upscaling DVD player, be prepared to experiment. Depending on the quality of the electronics at each end of the cable, picture quality may vary wildly between types of connection.

Many upscaling DVD players won't, for instance, output an HD signal over their component outputs, restricting you to HDMI. If yours allows it, it's worth comparing the quality of component to HDMI. You may find you actually prefer the slight analogue softness of the former.

System power

The life blood of any home-cinema system is the mains power that runs it. What you see onscreen and hear from your speakers is the juice supplied by the power companies, modified and turned into light and vibrations. And as strange as it may seem, this can be massively affected by an erratic mains supply or poor mains leads, especially those that come supplied with your kit.

When there's excess noise coming into a power inlet, it can filter through to your sensitive hi-fi and AV equipment. This is especially true of analogue equipment – crudely speaking, an amplifier takes the signal from a source component and adds more electricity to it to make it louder. If you have 'dirty' electricity, it can affect the performance of your equipment.

Products such as Isotek's Mira filter (£150) not only clean up your mains electricity signal, but will also act as surge protectors, preventing damage to your expensive equipment in the event of a mains spike. Improvement depends on how bad your mains connection is in the first place, but adding a mains filter and properly shielded mains cables can make a huge difference to the way your setup sounds and, to a lesser extent, looks onscreen – in most cases, more than the interconnects themselves. *iG*

113

Surround-sound audio explained

Don't know your Dolby Pro Logic II from your DTS-HD Master Audio? We explain just what all those formats mean

THX

You'll see the THX logo used in all sorts of contexts, but it isn't actually an audio format – rather a certification of quality awarded to cinemas and latterly domestic theatre and in-car audio products. It essentially aims to guarantee a standard of quality, regardless of the actual configuration used.

Surround-sound setups, or home theatre systems, are a common sight in modern living rooms. They usually consist of five speakers and a subwoofer, and are designed to create an immersive audio environment similar to that of a cinema. Games consoles, DVDs, Blu-ray and the now-defunct HD DVD use a variety of surround-sound formats to provide multichannel audio for all those speakers.

Digital and analogue

Surround sound actually pre-dates digital formats such as DVD. Original analogue formats such as Dolby Surround used a process called matrixing. This uses phase shifts in frequency to encode the surround-sound channels into a normal stereo soundtrack. You can still play it through a stereo amp or TV, but a compatible surround-sound amplifier can decode the hidden information and use it to recreate the multichannel surround soundtrack. Dolby Pro Logic II is the common matrixed surround-sound format, but its audio positioning, although effective, can't match up to that of discrete digital surround formats. Dolby Pro Logic amplifiers can also work with basic stereo soundtracks to give non-surround sources a wider sense of space.

Surround-sound branding

The most commonly used digital surround-sound format is Dolby Digital 5.1. This has five discrete audio channels: centre, front-left and front-right, rear-left and rear-right, plus a low-frequency effect (LFE) channel, which is only used for bass sound effects. Dolby Digital tracks are to be found on almost all DVD movie releases, with the movie's original multichannel soundtrack remastered and compressed to 448Kb/sec. Dolby's main competitor in both cinema and home theatre markets is Digital Theatre Sound (DTS). DTS soundtracks are considered superior in quality to Dolby Digital ones, but take up more space, usually 768Kb/sec. As such, DTS soundtracks are far less common due to restrictions on space – and the fact that Dolby Digital is a mandatory part of the DVD-Video format.

Dolby Digital and DTS soundtracks are output from the DVD player to a surround-sound decoding amplifier, commonly called an AV receiver (*see p105*), via optical or coaxial S/PDIF. The amp then decodes the digital audio and outputs it to your speakers.

Both companies have developed a wide array of surround-sound formats. You'll often see their logos plastered across the front of any AV receiver. Most of these formats, such as DTS-ES and Dolby Digital EX, add extra surround channels for either 6.1 or 7.1 setups. This is either achieved by matrixing them into the usual 5.1 channels, or preferably by adding new discrete channels. But none of these formats are widely supported on DVD, and have become relatively redundant since the advent of Blu-ray and HD DVD.

High-definition sound?

The large storage capacity of Blu-ray (and HD DVD) discs has allowed Dolby and DTS to boost the audio quality of surround soundtracks tremendously. Dolby TrueHD and DTS-HD Master Audio can both handle soundtracks of 18Mb/sec on Blu-ray. They use lossless compression, and are capable of flawlessly recreating the original master soundtrack with up to eight discrete channels of high-fidelity audio.

This is all dependent on the disc producer dedicating enough space to the audio, however, which can be an issue once you have multiple languages and special features to include. When space is an issue, 7.1-channel Dolby Digital Plus or eight-channel DTS-HD High Resolution Audio can be used instead, with maximum bit rates of up to 6Mb/sec depending on the disc format.

Despite these new high-resolution formats already appearing on discs, there have been issues with how to output them from early Blu-ray players. S/PDIF outputs and HDMI 1.1 ports used on these models aren't capable of dealing with these data-intensive formats. Instead, the soundtrack usually had to be mixed down into another format before being output. The latest disc players, games consoles and AV receivers support HDMI 1.3, though, which is fully compatible with all the latest formats. So, if you're buying an AV receiver, check it supports HDMI 1.3.

PC surround sound

For many years, PCs could only output surround sound through a series of analogue mini-jacks, which connected to specially designed PC speaker systems. Thankfully, many modern PCs have S/PDIF ports so you can output Dolby Digital or DTS soundtracks directly to an AV receiver. The latest range of graphics cards from ATi can also output audio through an HDMI converter, although they're only at HDMI 1.2 and so can't output the latest HD audio formats.

PC games haven't traditionally used home theatre surround-sound formats, although you can now buy sound cards that support Dolby Digital Live. These re-encode in real-time the surround sound from your game into 5.1 Dolby Digital, which you can then output using an S/PDIF to a surround-sound amp.

Dolby headphone and SRS

Having lots of speakers cluttering up your living room can be impractical or unsightly. However, there are a number of technologies that try to simulate surround sound using only two speakers. Sound Retrieval System (SRS) is the most commonly encountered. It's a psycho-acoustic effect that's designed to fool your ears into thinking the audio is bigger and more spacious, like listening to music in a large auditorium. It isn't universally effective with the small speakers often built into TV sets, but works better with

⮕ A breakdown of which formats you'll find on which discs

AUDIO CODEC	DVD			HD DVD			BLU-RAY		
	REQUIRED?	MAX CHANNELS	MAX BIT RATE	REQUIRED?	MAX CHANNELS	MAX BIT RATE	REQUIRED?	MAX CHANNELS	MAX BIT RATE
DOLBY DIGITAL	Mandatory	5.1	448Kb/sec	Mandatory	5.1	448Kb/sec	Mandatory	5.1	640Kb/sec
DTS	Optional	5.1	768Kb/sec	Mandatory	5.1	1.5Mb/sec	Mandatory	5.1	1.5Mb/sec
DOLBY DIGITAL PLUS	N/A	N/A	N/A	Mandatory	7.1	3Mb/sec	Optional	7.1	1.7Mb/sec
DTS-HD HIGH RESOLUTION AUDIO	N/A	N/A	N/A	Optional	8	3Mb/sec	Optional	8	6Mb/sec
DOLBY TRUEHD	N/A	N/A	N/A	Mandatory	8	18Mb/sec	Optional	8	18Mb/sec
DTS-HD MASTER AUDIO	N/A	N/A	N/A	Optional	8	18Mb/sec	Optional	8	24.5Mb/sec

proper hi-fi equipment at higher volumes. Note that SRS isn't a matrixing format with extra channels encoded, but rather an enhancement of the basic stereo signal.

If you want surround sound, but in the privacy of your head, you could try Dolby Headphone. This takes a 5.1 surround-sound signal and uses a room-modelling algorithm to reproduce it from a normal pair of stereo headphones. It gives a much greater sense of space than normal headphone listening, with the sources appearing to be located beyond the headphone cups around your ears.

DVD
All DVD players are required to support Dolby Digital, since the format is also a required part of the DVD-Video standard. DTS was only added to the DVD standard later and so isn't a mandatory requirement for discs, which also means that some older players don't support it. Check that any new DVD player you buy supports both formats and has an S/PDIF output to carry the audio to an AV receiver.

Blu-ray (and HD DVD)
These players should support all the key audio formats, including the latest lossless formats such as Dolby TrueHD. All HD DVD movies come with Dolby Digital Plus and Dolby TrueHD soundtracks, while Blu-ray discs vary more, with both Dolby TrueHD and DTS-HD Master Audio being optional, one or the other is usually supported.

But some early players aren't capable of outputting these formats unchanged to a compatible AV receiver. If you want the best surround-sound audio, make sure both your new player and your AV receiver are HDMI 1.3 compatible.

Games
The Xbox 360 and PlayStation 3 can both generate Dolby Digital 5.1 surround sound in real-time for games. This can then be output using either HDMI or S/PDIF to a compatible AV receiver. Both consoles also support Dolby Pro Logic II for matrixed surround sound using an analogue output. The Wii supports only Dolby Pro Logic II.

Broadcast
Many programmes broadcast in the UK have matrixed surround sound in their audio track, which a Dolby Pro Logic-compatible AV receiver can decode. But terrestrial broadcasts don't yet support discrete digital surround-sound formats. Subscription-based TV providers such as Virgin and Sky (see p76) broadcast many films with Dolby Digital 5.1 sound, and you can benefit from this by hooking up your set-top box to an AV receiver. ⓖ

HD projectors

Want a 100in HDTV for a fraction of the cost? Buy an HD projector and you can enjoy even bigger images than this

Look out for a projector with a well-featured remote control, or you'll be stuck poking at the onboard controls.

The lens will allow you to manually adjust focus and zoom independently, giving you more scope on positioning.

The bulb is the most expensive part of a projector's running costs, so check how much a replacement will cost.

Projectors can kick out plenty of heat (not to mention noise), so make sure there's plenty of airflow.

Many homes in the UK don't have living rooms big enough to accommodate a 42in or larger HDTV without it dominating the whole room. But an HD projector can magically conjure a cinema-sized image from a box that will hardly even be noticed when it's switched off and tucked in the corner.

If your walls are painted white, you can even get away with projecting straight onto them instead of buying a screen (although purists will baulk at this). Some projectors can even adjust their colours to compensate for projecting onto pale colours – so you may be able to stick with those magnolia walls after all. If you want to ceiling-mount a projector, it's worth noting that projectors will often come in white versions, for situations where a black case will be all too conspicuous.

Being choosy

If there's a limited distance between the projector and the screen (or wall) it will be projecting on to, yet you want the largest possible image, look for a model with a bigger optical zoom. Most zooms are 1.2x, which means the image size can be increased by around 20%. But some projectors have 2x zooms, which are able to produce a much larger image from the same throw distance.

The real question, though, is whether to choose a 720p or a 1080p model. You'll find 720p projectors considerably less expensive than their 1080p cousins, but they won't look as sharp, especially when you're talking about image sizes of 60-80in. Not surprisingly, 1080p is the ultimate choice if you can afford it, since this matches the resolution of Blu-ray movies as well as some high-definition TV broadcasts. Games consoles such as Microsoft's Xbox 360 and Sony's PlayStation 3 also support 1080p.

LCD vs DLP

Another consideration is the technology used. Most home-cinema projectors use either LCD or DLP systems. Both have their respective pros and cons, although newer LCD projectors have overcome the major disadvantage with the technology: the fact that older LCD panels used organic compounds that degraded over time and led to patches of colour on the resulting image. The latest models use inorganic materials that don't degrade, significantly prolonging their useful life.

Most DLP projectors, unlike LCD, don't have separate light paths for the primary colours, instead using a single path. Because of this, a colour wheel with red, green and blue segments is used, spinning so fast that your eye can't detect that each colour is being projected a fraction of a second after the other. But some people can see the individual colours when scanning their eyes across the image – known as the rainbow effect – and this can be very distracting. If possible, visit a store where you can try before you buy to see if it bothers you. 🄶

JVC DLA-HD1

Price:	£3800
Website:	www.jvc.co.uk
Rating:	★★★★★

There's a revolutionary new optical design in this projector that's turned the world of home cinema on its head. But all you need to know is that it means truly sensational picture quality. Amazingly deep black can appear side-by-side with extremely bright whites, since there's no need to reduce the light output during dark scenes to deliver more convincing blacks. JVC quotes a remarkably high contrast ratio of 15000:1 for the HD1, and we can believe it. The opening space battle from *Star Wars: The Revenge of the Sith*, for instance, has simply never looked better, with dazzlingly bright space ships fly whizzing by against an inky black outer space.

It also wows with its sharpness, putting its full HD native resolution to irresistible effect in both HD and SD, with virtually no apparent video noise. Colours also dazzling with their natural tones and vibrancy. It may struggle coping with the 150in screen of your dreams, but with the 70-140in screens more suited to domestic use, the HD1 is arguably the best way to blow nearly four grand we've ever come across!

SONY VPL-VW40

Price:	£2400
Website:	www.sony.co.uk
Rating:	★★★★☆

Considering the technology inside, this is a bargain. The neat diamond shape and elegant finish impress, as do its two HDMIs and 12V trigger output for motorised screens. Inside, the VW40 beats a full HD heart, with a claimed contrast ratio of 15000:1 via a dynamic iris system that adjusts the light let through the lens. It sounds promising, though in reality we struggled to make dark scenes look 100% convincing. Depending on your settings, black picture segments actually look black but contain little detail, or they'll look detailed but slightly grey and flat. Colours also look slightly pallid versus the best projectors for the money.

Fortunately the VW40 has two considerable saving graces: its extreme sharpness, and its total freedom from video noise. The crispness and texture of high definition pictures frequently takes your breath away, leaving many rivals looking fuzzy by comparison. But the real clincher is that the SXRD projection system frees those susceptible to DLP and LCD side effects, producing a picture that's incredibly pure.

VIEWSONIC PRO8100

Price:	£1900
Website:	www.viewsonic.com
Rating:	★★★★☆

The Pro8100's considerable bulk may reduce its living room appeal, but it wears its size well, and you can even choose from four colour options: black, burgundy, grey and white. And don't be alarmed by the performance out of the box – you can improve things massively with some relatively straightforward tweaking. Calling in the onboard Precision Colour System is enough to completely transform things, with vivid, natural colours and a marked improvement in sharpness, with HD pictures looking exceptionally crisp and full of texture – even when in motion.

It isn't entirely perfect: while you can use manual iris adjustment to have dark parts of the picture quite black by LCD standards, this comes at the expense of shadow detail, and the provided automatic iris system causes the picture to flicker distractingly at times. Pictures can also look rather noisy, especially with standard definition. Ultimately, if you favour acute subtlety and finesse, you may be better looking elsewhere. But there's no denying the talent this projector has for naked aggression and visual drama: there's little if anything else in this price bracket to match it.

INFOCUS X 10

Price:	£900
Website:	www.infocus.com
Rating:	★★★★★

This is outrageously cheap for a full HD DLP projector, but there's precious little sign of it. Its surprisingly large, rounded, black chassis is rather attractive, and it employs a novel mount upon which the main projector body can rotate and tilt to assist you in correct positioning. There are two HD-capable digital video inputs too.

And while the innards aren't cutting-edge, image quality doesn't suffer for it. For a sub-£1K projector, it produces the deepest blacks we've seen, while also being bright enough to make light scenes really sparkle. In fact, picture quality is nothing short of revelatory for the price. Colours are a remarkably accomplished, with rich saturation and consistently natural tones There's practically no noise in either standard- or high-definition sources, humbling projectors costing double. Moving objects don't pass by quite as fluidly or sharply as they might on more expensive projectors, and it is a touch noisy. We spotted some low-level DLP 'rainbow effect' too. But seriously, these downers simply can't distract from this being one of the finest sub-£1k home projectors you can buy.

INTRO | CHOOSING | BUYING | SETTING UP | ENJOYING HD | HD ON YOUR PC | EXPANSION | HD HOME

CHAPTER 8

HD home

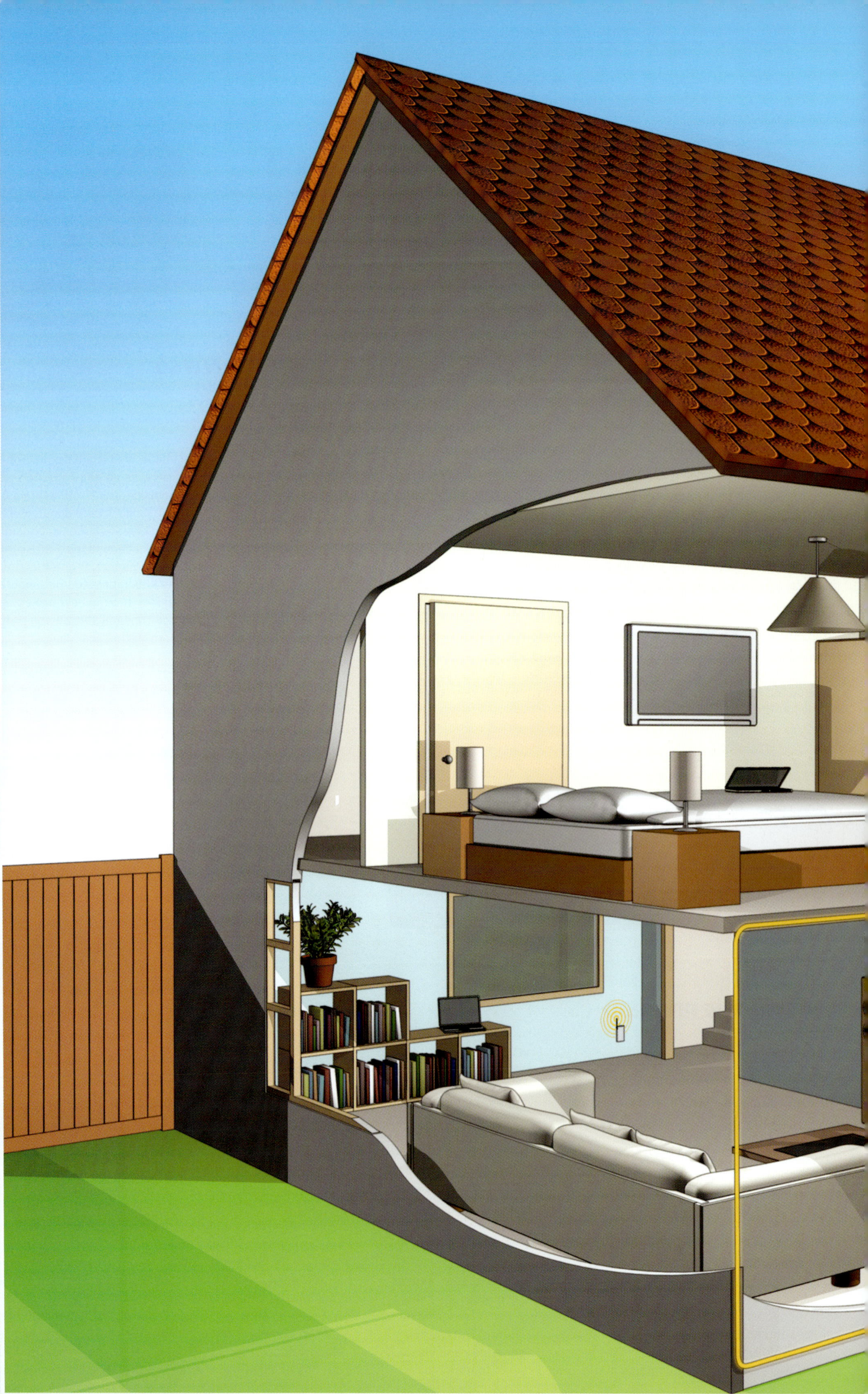

Why stop at just one room? There are plenty of opportunities to get HD content streaming all over the house these days, and if you have a wireless router already you're halfway there. From basic network storage to setting up centralised backup and streaming servers, we'll look at how to get a rock-solid HD network up and running in your home. And then, for good measure, we'll see how easy it is to create your own HD view of the world using the latest in camcorders. There's never been a better time for DIY HD.

Illo: Magic Torch

Setting up an HD-capable network

There are many ways to get HD videos from a hard disk to your living-room TV, but all require a network of some sort

With a top-quality screen and a high-definition source like a Sky+ box or an HD player, you may think you have everything you need for the ultimate viewing experience. But many people have other videos, too, sitting inconveniently on the hard disks of PCs and laptops around the house.

In fact, with the growth of video-on-demand services, the internet is now home to a gargantuan amount of content of a quality that is worthy of display on your HDTV. And the easiest way of getting to this content is to set up a network linking your TV to the other devices in your home using a wireless router.

Get connected

If you already have a broadband internet connection, many deals now come with a wireless router included. If not – or if, as with many ISPs, the provided router is a particularly cheap and underpowered model – it's simple to buy your own and set it up yourself (*see p122 for some suggestions*). You'll need to know what kind of internet connection you have: if your connection comes via the telephone line – as with most companies, such as Tiscali or Sky – you'll need an ADSL router; if your connection comes via a TV-style cable line – most commonly Virgin Media – you'll need a cable router.

Even if you have already been provided with a USB modem, don't worry about discarding it, since most of today's wireless routers have a modem integrated anyway, and you're likely to pay almost as much for a dedicated router without a modem. Most routers have an input for the data line, a wireless antenna to communicate with wireless PCs and laptops, as well as four Ethernet ports for connecting to devices via a cable. Some also come with a USB port, which is often used to easily transfer the necessary connection settings from the router to each client machine.

Going wireless

What type of router you choose will depend on the devices you want to connect to it. The 802.11 wireless communications standard comes in several flavours, each with progressively higher transfer speeds: the most widely used is currently 802.11g, which transfers data at a theoretical maximum rate of 54Mb/sec. It's backwards compatible with the 11Mb/sec 802.11b standard, but to have any chance of transferring HD content across your network you'll need 802.11g devices at all links in the chain – that's the router and each PC, laptop and any media-streaming device you want to use (*see p128*).

But the unfortunate truth is that HD video is very intensive to transfer: a 1080p H.264 file – the format used by many commercial HD discs and Sky HD broadcasts – can have a bit rate upwards of 50Mb/sec, while more compressed WMV9 files still need a network capable of transferring consistently above 8Mb/sec. To get this transfer rate from 802.11g, you'll need an absolutely ideal scenario in your home: line of sight (no walls) and a short distance between the video source, router and destination is a must; otherwise, you'll experience dropouts as the rate drops below the minimum threshold.

> " ...the internet is now home to a gargantuan amount of content worthy of display on your HDTV...

Hasty hardware

One solution lies in the newer 802.11n standard, which is currently in the troubled and long-winded process of being ratified. It adds to the previous standard by allowing for multiple-input multiple-output (MIMO) – basically more than one transmitter and receiver antenna to improve the signal – and will (theoretically) communicate at up to 248Mb/sec. The problem is that as 802.11n overlays multiple channels on the same frequencies, the interference between them increases massively. For example, 802.11b routers had 12 channels to choose from; 802.11g transmits only on channels 1, 6 and 12 to give each other enough headroom; 802.11n uses just two, making interference a real problem if you're not careful.

Impatient for the ratification, many manufacturers have brought out 802.11 draft-n routers and network cards for PCs and notebooks, although the current crop of media-streaming devices and wireless NAS boxes is largely limited to 802.11g. There are also other standards that aim to fill the gap: Super G and MIMO both perform better than the basic 802.11g, and may be options if you have a larger house or thick walls.

Wired for HD

The other option is to use good old-fashioned wires, either partially or throughout your network. Drilling through a wall may seem an extreme solution to transfer your data through brick, but it gets the desired result. It can be messy to install, but once it's in you won't have the worries that many people have with wireless.

Alternatively, you can pick and choose the links to wire: for example, if you had a draft-n router receiving video from a draft-n laptop, you could then run a wired line from the router to your streaming device to eliminate the 802.11g bottleneck.

Another option is powerline networking, as explained on p123. There are several grades of adapter available and, if you ensure you buy adapters capable of a high enough transfer rate, you can have HD video streaming around your house reliably and consistently. They should also be considered if you have a house with particularly thick walls, or a layout that puts too great a distance between the router and the farthest rooms.

They aren't particularly cheap and need to be used in pairs, though, so the downside is that kitting out a whole house will cost considerably more than a wireless, or possibly even wired, network.

Quality of service

Whatever method you choose, we recommend you use a router that supports Quality of Service (QoS). This allows a router to prioritise different types of network traffic based on its needs: for example, if you have something downloading in the background but also want to stream a video to your media receiver, you want your router to know that the video should be given all the bandwidth it needs for its duration; otherwise, the download could interfere with it. With HD video requiring such high transfer rates, it's vital that the router keeps the video streaming as quickly as possible. ⓖ

121

Routers

A basic router costs peanuts these days, but not all will cope with the demands of HD streaming wirelessly

ADSL

CABLE

UPnP

Standing for Universal Plug 'n' Play, this is a set of protocols for sharing data (such as video) between devices over a network, and allowing one UPnP device the ability to configure another. The UPnP AV variant is supervised by manufacturers in the DLNA (Digital Living Network Alliance), and pays specific attention to sharing audiovisual content.

➦ D-LINK DIR-855

Price:	£154
Internet:	www.dlink.co.uk
Rating:	★★★★☆

For the ultimate in HD streaming performance, routers like this run two Wi-Fi networks in parallel – one in the 2.4GHz band and one in the 5GHz – allowing one to be used entirely for streaming HD video without interfering with each other.

The DIR-855 is filled to the gunnels with other features too. Its WISH QoS system allows you to prioritise certain traffic types by application – VOIP, Windows Media Player and so on – guest zones can be set up, both white and black lists are supported for website filtering and an OLED screen allows you to view settings at a glance. Performance is very quick, though there's no ADSL modem built in.

The only downside is the expense: £154 is a lot of cash for a router, plus to take full advantage of the dual band feature you'll need to buy an extra dual-band wireless PC adapter.

➦ BELKIN N1 VISION

Price:	£95
Internet:	www.belkin.com/uk
Rating:	★★★★☆

Belkin's N1 Vision might be expensive, but it's crammed features. Not only is this a fast, 802.11n draft 2.0 certified router, but it also boasts four gigabit Ethernet ports and a built-in ADSL modem and a host of unusual features.

The most noticeable is its LCD screen, which provides information about download and upload speeds, download and upload totals, plus details on the wireless security settings and the names of any connected devices.

You can also set up a guest account using the screen and its controls, so you can provide visitors with secure access to your network without compromising your own passwords. And first time set-up is fantastically easy thanks to an embedded on-device wizard. It's pricy, but for those wanting all the features around, it's an attractive option.

➦ LINKSYS WAG160N

Price:	£58
Internet:	www-uk.linksys.com
Rating:	★★★★★

The unusually sleek looking WAG160N is designed to fit seamlessly into any domestic environment. Its aerials don't stick out but are embedded into the chassis, lending it cleaner lines than most. But don't be fooled by the looks; this is also a great performer and stuffed with features. It's compliant with the latest draft of the 802.11n standard (2.0), and certified by the WiFi Alliance to make sure it'll work with other 'n' devices. It's reliable and fast, too, has an ADSL modem built in and around the back there are four Ethernet ports for connecting wired network devices.

The best thing about this router, however, is it's a breeze to set up, and bundled network management software – EasyLink Advisor. This presents your network and all the devices on it in a super-clear graphical manner that's far superior to Windows' own confusing tools.

ADSL

➦ TRENDNET TEW-637AP

Price:	£45
Internet:	http://trendnetuk.com
Rating:	★★★★☆

If the thought of installing a new router or modem fills you with dread, this unusual device from Trendnet might take your fancy. Plug it into a spare network port on your current router (wireless or not), run through the setup routine provided on a CD in the box, and you'll have a fast, reliable wireless-n network in a matter of minutes.

The beauty of this device is in its simplicity, so there's not a lot else to it. There are no Ethernet ports and no modem. But it's a certified draft 2.0 device, which means it has all of the same features you'd expect of a full-blown media router – including WPA2 encryption, QOS and WPS for security setup at the touch of a button.

Installing the Trendnet involves extra cable clutter, but it's a very easy, hassle-free way of upgrading your network to wireless-n, and it's relatively cheap too.

802.11n

Powerline networking

Wireless network not reliable enough? Then use your existing mains power wiring to create a network

Wireless networks, even those using the latest standards, can be unreliable or fail to deliver enough speed to handle HD video. The size of your house and the construction of interior walls can affect speed and range, and you may find that your router's wireless signal simply isn't strong enough to reach where you want it to go.

If that's the case, you could trail a long network cable from your router to your digital media adapter – or you could use your existing mains wiring instead. Many manufacturers produce adapters that plug into any free wall socket and can transmit data to each other using the powerlines. In most houses, the wiring is all on the same circuit, so communication is possible between any two sockets throughout the house.

Wired for video

Although some manufacturers use proprietary technologies, most use the HomePlug standard, so you can buy various brands and they will all communicate. There are three main speed ratings: 15Mb/sec, 85Mb/sec and 200Mb/sec (also known as HomePlug AV). These are theoretical maximums, and the actual throughput is typically less than half these figures, depending tremendously on the quality of your mains wiring and the distance between the adapters. The surest way to ensure enough speed for HD video is to opt for HomePlug AV, as they can handle the 25Mb/sec required for skip-free HD playback.

Simple setup

Connect one HomePlug adapter to your router using a standard network cable, and do the same with the other and your digital media receiver. A connection will then be automatically established. You'll also want to use the manufacturer's software to enable security features that prevent any neighbours from latching onto your network via their own HomePlug adapters.

Some adapters plug directly into the socket, while others have a separate power cable, which is neater if the socket is in plain view. The main disadvantage of powerline networking, though, is the cost. Even when bought in pairs, HomePlug AV adapters cost around £60 each, so it's worth trying wireless networking first. You may find that you can get away with 85Mb/sec adapters but, unfortunately, there's no way to find out whether you can without testing a pair to see if HD video plays smoothly.

ROUTERS

Routers with HomePlug technology are now starting to appear. These are able to use the router's power cable for networking as well, so only use one power socket. Also, you don't have to use HomePlugs in pairs – any number can communicate together. Just be aware that if they all need to communicate at once the speed will drop, since the bandwidth is shared between all the devices.

➡ ZYXEL HOMEPLUG AV PLA-400

Price	£129
Internet	www.zyxel.com
Rating	★★★★☆

ZyXEL's HomePlug AV adapters don't plug directly into a socket, but come with reasonably long power cables so you can hide them out of sight – and they even have wall-mounting holes for tidiness.

They're smartly finished in silver and black, and have obvious LEDs on the front so you can see when data is being sent and received. Setting up the adapters is easy – just plug them in and run the setup utility on your PC. This lets you choose a password to encrypt data sent between the adapters.

The PLA-400s are capable of around **32Mb/sec** of sustained throughput, which is more than enough for a single HD video. This price is for a pair – not exactly cheap, but they certainly do the job.

➡ DEVOLO DLAN 200 AV HOMEPLUG STARTER KIT

Price	£105
Internet	www.devolo.co.uk
Rating	★★★★★

The dLAN 200 AV plugs are available either in 'plug' format or as separate units like the ZyXELs. The latter cost £15 more and go by the name of AVdesk.

The kit includes two network cables, and there's a similar configuration utility that you can run if you want to secure your powerline network. It's worth noting that HomePlugs supporting the 200Mb/sec standard aren't backwards compatible with 85Mb/sec and 14Mb/sec standards, though.

In our testing, the dLAN 200 AV managed **38Mb/sec** – a perfectly good performance. Even better, the Devolo's performance doesn't fluctuate when used on a four-way plug, or when interfering devices are plugged in.

➡ NETGEAR POWERLINE HDXB101

Price	£85
Internet	www.netgear.co.uk
Rating	★★★★☆

Although these adapters boast the same 200Mb/sec speed as ZyXEL and Devolo, they don't use the HomePlug standard, instead working on Netgear's proprietary system.

The plugs are large enough to prevent the use of adjacent sockets, although setup is otherwise similar to HomePlugs. You may need to enable the coexistence mode to allow the plugs to work on a mains circuit with other HomePlug adapters, though.

Used on their own, the HDXB101s managed a decent 40Mb/sec, but switch to coexistence mode and this drops to 27Mb/sec, so is best avoided. Performance is also adversely affected when used in multiplug adapters and when other devices are plugged in.

Network-attached storage

Want to add some storage to your network?
You'll be needing some network attached storage then...

USB ports on the back allow you to add more storage capacity to your NAS, or adding a disk to back up to. Some will also let you read from USB flash drives, or add a printer to share on the network.

Most NAS drives will have a power button. They're designed to be left on all the time, although most can be set to allow the disk to spin down when not in use.

Many drives will come with a fan to keep the hard disk inside cool. Some of these are noisier than others, though – if that bothers you, opt for one that's passively cooled.

The network port will be either fast ethernet or gigabit ethernet, which, confusingly, is the faster of the two. As such, it's a better bet for streaming HD video around the place.

The possibilities offered by HD media-streaming devices (*see p128*) are fantastic, but many people will baulk at having to leave their PC switched on all the time to supply them. Not only is it bad news for your bank balance, it's bad for the environment, and an awful waste when no-one's sat in front of the PC. Luckily, there's an alternative that does away with the PC: a network-attached storage (NAS) device.

Just a disk
A NAS device is essentially a hard disk housed within its own self-contained and properly cooled box, along with a power supply. Not all NAS boxes suit our needs, but if you check the specifications before you buy you'll find many that have their own UPnP server installed, which means they can communicate with a media receiver directly.

But the key point is that rather than attaching to your computer via USB like most external hard disks, a NAS device only needs to be able to access your network; in fact, it needn't be situated anywhere near a PC at all. Instead, you have two choices: either connect it directly to your router via an ethernet port or have it connect wirelessly to your home network, meaning you can tuck the box discreetly away anywhere in reach of a power socket.

Central station
While a NAS device needs to remain powered on while streaming your media, it consumes a fraction of the power of a PC or notebook, and can be extremely useful in other ways, too. It helps you to keep organised by gathering the files from all of your PCs onto one central hard disk, for example, where they'll be immune to viruses and system crashes that may sneak up unexpectedly.

Any computers on the network can access the NAS box just like a normal hard disk, and family members can be given their own password-protected partitions on the disk, so there's also no danger of the kids accessing anything they shouldn't. And then there's the most obvious bonus of extra hard disk space – room for those all-important backups and archives; with hundreds of videos, MP3s and photos on most people's PCs these days, it makes a NAS device a great investment for any home.

➔ MAXTOR SHARED STORAGE II

Price	**£140**
Internet	**www.maxtor.co.uk**
Rating	★★★★★

With 500GB of capacity coming from a single hard disk (300GB and larger 1TB units are also available), the Maxtor is the perfect starting point for getting your home storage going. It's easily expandible, too, with two USB ports at the rear for adding on extra drives, or even attaching a printer.

The Shared Storage II is also a UPnP media server, so will work with most media receivers, and also comes with an iTunes DAAP (Digital Audio Access Protocol) server, so any music stored on the drive will be available to anyone using Apple's iTunes software on your network. There's also a handy Drag and Sort feature, which can automatically organise files into the correct folders on the disk by type, ensuring all your video or photos end up in one place.

Its speedy performance means there shouldn't be any problem with several people streaming content from it simultaneously, and even when it's working hard it's near silent. But the best part is the price, which is just a fraction more than you'd pay for a basic external disk.

➔ HP MEDIA VAULT PRO MV5020

Price	**£200**
Internet	**www.hp.com/uk**
Rating	★★★★★

For sheer value, it's difficult to beat this smart little black box. There are two slide-out drawers behind the door at the front, one of which comes fitted with a 500GB disk as standard, to which you can simply add another. If you want to add more, there are two USB sockets in which to plug in an external hard disk. For peace of mind, you can split the storage on extra disks in half, so they're mirrored in case one fails. There's also a utility included that will automatically back up each of your connected PCs.

Other features include a server that handily consolidates any iTunes music libraries into one place. There are also remote access features, so you can access your server files over the internet from anywhere, and an online backup option, although the latter is via a rather pricey subscription, costing around £75 a year for 40GB.

It's also too noisy for our liking, and it could be easier to set up. But if you've got somewhere out of the way to put it, it's a great value and flexible option for our network.

DVICO TVIX HD M-6500A

An alternative to using a NAS box and a media streamer, this device acts somewhat like a combination of the two. The 'barebones' version (£299) comes without a hard disk, but you can get various options, up to £500 for a 1TB disk installed – or you can install your own.

At the back, you'll find an HDMI v1.3 socket for connecting directly to your TV, and an Ethernet port to hook it up to your network – a wireless dongle is also available if there's no port near your TV. USB ports let you plug in flash drives for playback or transfer, as well as for connecting to PC to add files to the hard drive, if fitted. Setting it up to play content from over the network is rather trickier, with a complicated configuration procedure and limited control over which folders it will access.

Format support is impressive, and it's able to playback just about anything that you'll commonly find (including ripped DVDs). It's an incredibly versatile device – and you can expand its talents even further with a TV tuner, turning it into a PVR. It's pricey, but there's no arguing with its flexibility. See _www.kjglobal.co.uk_ for more.

➔ SYNOLOGY DISK STATION DS508

Price	**£658**
Internet	**www.asus.com**
Rating	★★★★☆

You can never have enough storage, and this imposing-looking NAS device will give you it by the bucketload. This price doesn't include any disks, but for sheer industrial levels of performance and capacity potential, it's a winner.

Up to five drives can be installed, giving you a maximum of five terabytes to play with – hundreds of Blu-ray discs worth – even if you opt for one of the modes that provides data security or enhanced speed at the cost of capacity.

It's unlikely that only the most ambitious HD setups will need the latter though, as this is one of the fastest drives we've seen, and should cope with anything you throw at it.

There are also UPnP and iTunes servers built-in, as well as a BitTorrent downloader that can handle peer-to-peer downloads without needing a computer left on. The ambitious can also use it to host websites and file download servers. It even directly supports network-based cameras.

It's massive overkill for most, but if you're after the ultimate in network storage, it's an excellent choice.

Windows Home Server

Like a sort of Super NAS, Home Server brings a huge number of benefits to the modern connected home – here are just a few

A NAS disk is great for getting computer-based movies, music and photos on your network, but there's another option – setting up your own server. It may not sound like it, but it can be very simple to do. You could do a lot worse than to get a box with Microsoft's *Windows Home Server* software on. There are a few models to choose from (see opposite for some of them), but they all do much the same job – storing your data in one place, as well as offering some other intriguing features, all managed from a simple interface on your PC.

Not just NAS
Once you've plugged it into your broadband router, Home Server can store files from your computer in the same way as a NAS box, which you can then access with media receivers (*see p128*) or any computer connected to it.

Where Home Server wins over most NAS boxes, though, is that they can have several physical disks in them, and you can set important data to be copied onto both (known as folder duplication). So if one disk decides to die, your precious media files won't go with it.

Media streaming
Home Server also has a UPnP-compatible media server in it, so you use it to store music, photos and videos, and access them from any other compatible device, such as a dedicated media PC or a media receiver.

> Home Server makes sharing all your media around the house a doddle.

System backup
If you have a PC or two in your house, Home Server can also back these up automatically (including any music or video

you have on there). This can be set to run overnight so that you've always got everything safely backed up. Then, if (or when) disaster strikes, you can either restore individual files or your whole computer, as needed.

All you can eat
The other huge benefit over most NAS drives is that you can add as much storage to your server as you like. Most units will let you easily pop another hard disk inside, but you can also plug in external disks, which you can expand whenever you want, as extra storage is simply added to a 'pool'.

Playing away
You can even get to your files when you're away from home. Using your own personalised web address, you can log in from anywhere in the world and download or upload anything you want, or even log on remotely to one of your computers. Windows Home Server happily takes care of all the complicated bits behind the scenes, making the whole process surprisingly simple.

If you're feeling a bit more ambitious, you can even host your own website. That may not sound like much fun, but think about it: you can use it to store your own photo gallery, a download page for your old band's music, or a personal list of favourite website links that you can access from anywhere. The possibilities are endless. See *www.microsoft.com* for more details.

⊕ HP MEDIASMART SERVER

Price	£450
Internet	www.hp.com/uk
Rating	★★★★★

The MediaSmart Server comes in two configurations, with the difference between them being hard disk capacity. The EX470 has 500GB, but the EX475 trumps it with 1TB, split over two disks to make use of the folder-duplication features.

Open the hinged front door and you'll find the four drive bays, at least two of which will be free for you to add your own hard disks. It's a simple job of pulling out a drawer, putting in the disk and then replacing the caddy. There are also four USB ports to add external disks if that isn't enough.

HP also adds its Photo Webshare software to the package, which allows you to host a sophisticated photo- and video-sharing website from your home server. You can create accounts for friends and family, and allow them to upload their own photos, or comment on yours. There's also an iTunes server built in, so that any media stored can be made visible to anyone using iTunes on your network.

⊕ FUJITSU SIEMENS SCALEO 1900

Price	£400
Internet	www.fujitsu-siemens.co.uk
Rating	★★★★★

We can't quite decide whether the Scaleo looks like a projector or a particularly attractive suitcase. Either way, it packs a lot into a relatively small space. You've got the option of either a single 500GB drive (the Scaleo 1500) or this, the dual-drive, with a total of four internal drive bays to fill. There are also two USB ports at the front, with a further two at the back. What we really like, though, are the two e-SATA ports, which are the latest high-speed hard disk interface, and particularly good news for high data-rate streaming such as HD video.

As with the other units here, there's also the fastest gigabit Ethernet standard on board to keep video flowing smoothly, although you'll need a compatible router to get the best from it (see p122). Fujitsu Siemens also imbues the Scaleo with power-management software that allows the server to be 'always available' rather than always on, helping to keep down its power consumption.

⊕ TRANQUIL PC T2-WHS-A3 HARMONY

Price	£350
Internet	www.tranquilpc.co.uk
Rating	★★★★☆

It may look a little bit like an old video recorder, but this is one of the best Home Servers we've seen. First of all, the only sound you'll hear from the industrially sturdy chassis is the subtle clickety-clack of the hard disks, as it's entirely passively cooled – so no fan noise. It's also appealingly efficient, consuming around half the power of the HP MediaSmart server. And the manufacturer also pledges to offset its running cost carbon footprint for the first five years.

There's the option to add another hard disk when you buy, to take advantage of Home Server's duplication features, or you can add your own later. You also have the option of different cases – the desk style seen here, plus rack-mount and even floor – and wall-mount varieties. Given that it needs to be sited by an Ethernet port, the Tranquil's bulk could be an issue, but its silent, efficient running and well engineered finish count for a lot.

Media receivers

Want to get to your digital content anywhere in the house? You can, with the latest media-streaming devices

EXTENDERS

If you're running Windows Vista with Windows Media Center, a Media Center Extender could be the easiest way of getting PC-based files onto your TV.

Until recently, the Xbox 360 was the only Media Center Extender in the UK. However, we've now started to see the release of standalone boxes, which don't have the noisy fans of the Xbox 360 (or its price tag). Wireless networking lets them keep up with HD video streams, with support for DivX and XviD usually thrown in.

Computers are great for storing masses of video and audio without any of those pesky jewel cases or shiny discs cluttering up the place. But if you've built up a large collection of digital videos, music and photos, the good news is that they're not simply trapped on a hard disk.

Rather than kitting out each room of the house with a PC, you can now buy slim, lightweight boxes that act somewhere between a DVD player and a computer – connecting to your TV but playing back computer-based content from either your PC or network-attached storage box (see p124).

It's fairly early days, but there are still plenty such devices to choose from, each offering different features, including the PlayStation 3 (PS3) and Xbox 360 games consoles. Many can also double up as your DVD player: the PS3 also plays back Blu-ray discs, while Microsoft used to sell an add-on HD DVD drive for the Xbox 360 for less than £100.

But choosing the right video streamer can be tricky – the video format support in particular is a potential minefield for the unwary, so make sure it supports the files you're interested in. We've run the rule over a few of the best over the page.

Wireless, and why not?

Many of these streamers handle HD videos in formats such as WMV-HD, DivX and H.264, and although none guarantees to stream them wirelessly, you might well get away with it. You'll need to run an ethernet cable to be sure, but if that's out of the question there are other options. One is to invest in a pair of HomePlug adapters (see p123) and piggyback onto your mains wiring as a network.

A cheaper option is to look for a video streamer that can play files locally, either from an internal hard disk or externally from a USB flash drive, hard disk or DVD. This isn't ideal, though, as it means your videos aren't stored in a central location – a crucial factor if you plan to have multiple video streamers in the home.

File formats

If you want to watch DivX and XviD files – currently, the most common formats found on the internet – your options are limited. There are ways to convert DivX and XviD videos to other formats on-the-fly, but these can lead to a drop in quality. Apple's TV has the most limited support, but if you already have a large iTunes library and are happy to buy videos from the iTunes store it's still one of the best options – and its interface looks sublime on a good HD setup.

Game, set and match

Even if you don't particularly want a games console, both the Xbox 360 and PS3 also have their advantages as video streamers. The Xbox 360 is a Media Center Extender (see left), which effectively lets you link to a PC running either XP

> ## It's important to choose a player that matches the audio and video connections on your TV and hi-fi

Media Center Edition or Vista Media Center. You get exactly the same interface on your TV, and do everything as if you were sat using the media centre directly: make use of any digital TV tuners installed to watch Freeview channels, set scheduled recordings or view video stored on its hard disk.

The PS3, on the other hand, has a Blu-ray drive, so can replace your existing DVD player as well as playing Blu-ray movie discs. It also has a media card reader for playing files locally and four USB ports, so you can plug in a keyboard and mouse for even more flexibility.

Getting physical

It's important to choose a player that matches the audio and video connections on your TV and hi-fi, since adapters aren't usually included and can be expensive. HDMI is the most convenient interface, as it carries both video and audio in one cable. Alternatively, look for component outs for the best quality. You'll get the best audio from a digital S/PDIF interface, but make sure your amplifier has a matching input, since there are two types: optical and coaxial.

Lastly, don't forget about noise. All the units over the page

(save for the Xbox and PS3) are essentially silent, since they don't have any fans. The PS3's low whoosh is easily masked when listening to music, playing games or watching videos, but the Xbox 360's din could prove its undoing unless you make sure it is placed well away from where you're sitting.

Are you being served?

Media streamers need to get their files from somewhere, and that can be either a PC, a NAS box or the latest Windows Home Server products (see p126). If it's the first of these, you'll have a choice of using several different pieces of software. Most receivers will come with their own server included, but you can use Windows Media Connect (built into Windows Media Player) or take a third-party option. One such option is TVersity – a free media server, available from http://tversity.com. The advantage of TVersity in particular is its ability to transcode video on-the-fly. So even if your video streamer doesn't support a particular video format, the chances are that TVersity can transcode it to a format it does support. This is done on-demand, so there's no need to convert the file before playing it.

The quality of this transcoded video will depend on the power of the PC that TVersity is running on, although you can alter the resolution manually until you find the optimal setting for your system. You'll need a fairly beefy dual-core CPU to keep HD video looking good. Read on to see which receiver is right for you. Ⓖ

Lounge lizards: getting all your PC's video content to your HDTV is becoming easier as more media receivers are coming onto the market.

Media receivers

Here, we look at five boxes that will fix up your TV and your computer. It could be a match made in heaven...

● MICROSOFT XBOX 360 ELITE

Price	£230
Internet	www.xbox.com
Rating	★★★★☆

We've already seen that the Xbox 360 is a highly accomplished games console (see p72), but it's also a brilliant media receiver. Not only will it play back content from other computers and network-attached storage boxes (as well as from its 120GB hard disk or from USB drives), but it will also integrate beautifully with the Windows Media Center (see p128) application to give one of the best options around.

If you don't own a PC with Media Center installed, the built-in Windows Media Connect is used to stream media to the console from a PC. The menu is a little quirky but works well, and there are some good-looking photo slideshows, too.

It's highly annoying that the 802.11g wireless adapter costs a staggering £50, although we've found the Xbox's HD streaming more forgiving than most once it's fitted, and there's Gigabit Ethernet built in, too. The DVD-ROM can't match the PS3's Blu-ray, but it can still upscale DVDs well, and there's HDMI onboard too. You might also be able to pick up a bargain HD DVD drive for it too, as well as some very cheap disks.

The disappointments come with slightly patchy DivX and XviD support, although you can watch TV programmes recorded with Media Center. There's also an update available to give you MPEG4 and AAC support – handy for H.264 HD video files, and new media-related features are added fairly frequently..

The Xbox 360 would much more attractive for media streaming if it weren't for its one major flaw: it's noisier than most PCs. But if you can live with that, it's a great choice.

● SONY PLAYSTATION 3

Price	£300
Internet	www.sony.co.uk
Rating	★★★★☆

Okay, the PlayStation 3 isn't cheap, but then it blows everything else on this page out of the water when it comes to features. Quite apart from its many qualities as a media receiver and its scintillating gaming capabilities, it also betters the competition by including a very capable Blu-ray drive.

Another bonus is built-in 802.11g Wi-Fi and even Bluetooth. It's good to see an HDMI port in addition to a proprietary AV output, and there are also optical S/PDIF and Gigabit Ethernet interfaces too. USB ports can be used to charge the wireless controller, or to plug in a USB hard disk or flash drive from which to watch content.

Inside is an 40GB hard disk and you can also use this to store game data, music, photos and video. Format support includes MPEG-1, -2 and -4 (H.264 and AVCHD), but not DivX or XviD.

Its menus aren't quite as easy to navigate as the Xbox's, particularly when browsing the PlayStation store. But like Apple TV, it's simple to watch movie trailers, and there's even a built-in web browser, which works well with the wireless controller. You can even plug in a standard USB keyboard and mouse. And, while the PS3 isn't silent, it's certainly quieter than the Xbox 360 in full flow.

Viewed simply as a video streamer, the PS3 isn't amazing value, but the Blu-ray player alone makes it worth the price. If you're not bothered about that, the Xbox is cheaper and – when paired with a Media Center PC – offers the best video-streaming experience you'll find.

SLINGCATCHER

Price	**£217**
Internet	www.uk.slingmedia.com
Rating	★★★☆☆

It may look like Darth Vader's garage, but the Slingcatcher houses some rather nice technology of its own. Rather than simply talking to media stored on the network, it can handle content from a couple of different sources. If you've got a Slingbox (*see p133*), it can 'catch' its stream and display it directly on a TV via its HDMI ourput, either on the same network (in HD resolutions), or over the internet from a remote location. Or, you can use the SlingProjector software to stream either some or all of your PC or laptop's screen to your TV, enabling you to do anything you can on your computer, such as web browsing, watching YouTube, or catching up with the BBC's iPlayer – a nifty trick. It will also play media from an attached USB flash or hard drive, supporting the H.264, DviX and XviD codecs. Finally, there's the ability to stream content from your PC, albeit indirectly, using the SlingSync utility to automatically synchronise files from selected folders on your PC to a USB storage device.

Like the Slingbox, it's a niche device, but for those that can use its unique features, it's a brilliant and intriguingly innovative piece of kit. So now you can buy that luxury holiday villa without getting another Sky+ subscription.

LINKSYS DMA 2200

Price	**£200**
Internet	www-uk.linksys.com
Rating	★★★★☆

Like the Xbox 360 (*see left*), this is one of the few Media Center Extenders on the market, connecting to computers running certain versions of Windows Vista and giving you access to the same media on that PC – including streaming live TV or recorded programmes, music, video and photos. You can also access Media Center's PVR features.

For those without a Media Center PC, it can also work with Windows Media Connect to access the media on most PCs, as well as on hard disks or flash drives plugged into its USB ports. But there's also an 1080p upscaling DVD player, which takes advantage of the HDMI output. It also supports audio CDs, MP3 files, WMA and DivX video.

Given a good connection, the 802.11n Wi-Fi on board can comfortably cope with HD video streams, although it's slightly fussy when it comes to signal strength. The interface is also a touch sluggish at times – especially when connecting to a wireless network – but it's easy to use.

For those without the right back-end to connect it to, this is an expensive DVD player with some clever network features in. And there's no denying that the multi-talented Xbox 360 is much better value, albeit significantly noisier. But for those with the right network, it's a decent choice.

APPLE TV

Price	40GB, £185; 160GB, £270
Internet	www.apple.com/uk
Rating	★★★★☆

There are no buttons aon this lovely little slab of metal and plastic – it's controlled entirely by the tiny Apple remote. Plug it in, hook it up to your TV via HDMI and a simple setup connects to a wired or wireless network, via the built-on 802.11n. The interface is simply gorgeous; crisp and clean with large, easily readable text, and it's quick, too. You can watch film and TV trailers streamed straight from the iTunes store for free, or buy TV programmes (such as *Heroes* and *Desperate Housewives*) for £1.89 per episode, albeit in a distinctly standard-definition format in the UK. There's also integration with video-sharing website *YouTube*.

But it isn't perfect. First, you'll need to have an iTunes library (and account) set up on your PC or Mac in order to access photos, video and music, and it also means that video format support is limited, with QuickTime or H.264/MPEG-4 files supported, and hit-and-miss even then.

The built-in hard disk means you don't always need a computer switched on to view content on it, but the 40GB version is limited and the 160GB version pricey. If you run a Mac, it's an easier options, and it's particularly attractive to iPhone and iPod Touch users, who can use Apple's Remote app to control music playback over a Wi-Fi network.

Digital home devices and remotes

Once you're all networked up, there are masses of other entertainment options, such as these...

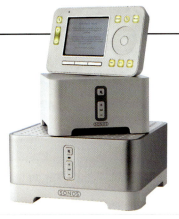

SONOS

Price	From £650
Internet	www.sonos.com
Rating	★★★★★

To round off your entertainment experience, there's nothing to beat a multiroom music system. A few years ago, this would have cost thousands of pounds, but the birth of digital music and wireless networking now means you can use a system like Sonos to easily pipe music around the house for less than a grand.

The sound quality is sensational, too, with both digital and analogue outputs present, plus inputs, so you can route your record deck or HD audio somewhere else in the house. Each wirelessly equipped ZonePlayer will play a different music stream (or internet-based radio) if you wish, or you can group them together to play the same track all around the house in perfect sync. The standalone wireless controller is a masterpiece of design, too. While it isn't exactly cheap, this system is our top choice for music lovers.

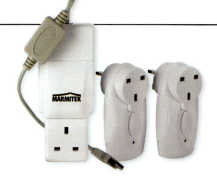

HARMONY HOME AUTOMATION STARTER KIT

Price	£150
Internet	www.simplyautomate.co.uk
Rating	★★★☆☆

Fancy living like The Jetsons? Sadly, this kit doesn't supply the hover car, but it will get you on the first rung of the home-automation ladder. Part of a huge range of products that can control everything from your home security to central heating, the home control kit will start you off modestly with a couple of light dimmers. You can then set up a schedule, so your PC will automatically switch each module to the required setting.

We're not crazy about the clunky software, but once you have a single button that switches on the TV, dims the lights and turns on your Blu-ray player it all feels surprisingly like the future. You can also buy extra modules that allow you to use a remote control rather than mouse and keyboard, and that's when we really start to warm to the concept... or is that the central heating coming on? Either way, this is a solid starter kit.

LOGITECH SQUEEZEBOX DUET

Price	£280
Internet	www.logitech.com
Rating	★★★★☆

This latest addition to the Squeezebox family is a real stunner. The sleek design will blend in just about anywhere, and it's beautifully built too. Connected to your computer (either a PC or Mac) via a Wi-Fi network, you can use multiple receivers and controllers, which can all operate independently, or together in one alight 'party mode'. Annoyingly, party animals will have to set that part up on the included SqueezeCenter computer software, rather than the remote, but it's a small inconvenience in the big scheme of things. At £280, it's not exactly cheap. But it does come with some excellent features – including internet radio and digital audio outputs. If investing in the more versatile Sonos system (*see above*) doesn't appeal, there's nothing in this price range to touch it.

SLING MEDIA SLINGBOX PRO

Price	£180
Internet	http://uk.slingmedia.com
Rating	★★★★☆

If you never want to be away from your video, the Slingbox Pro will be your new best friend, taking any video stream, digitising it and then broadcasting it to your home network. It can also transmit TV onto the internet, where you can access it via a broadband connection anywhere in the world. You can even use it to control your set-top box remotely.

The access software is compatible with both Macs and PCs, and you can even buy extra software for some mobile phones. There's an HD input on the back (sadly, only component – there's no HDMI), although even the fastest broadband connections will leave it some way off true HD resolutions. Not everyone will find a use for the Slingbox – especially at this price – but for those that can use it, it will be a godsend.

MICROSOFT MEDIA CENTER REMOTE

Price	£25
Internet	www.microsoft.com
Rating	★★★★☆

If you're running a PC with Windows XP Media Center, Vista Home Premium or Ultimate, this will be £25 well spent. Install the infrared receiver to a spare USB port and then you can use this well-designed remote to control Windows Media Center (*see p86*) or Windows Media Player, skipping around tracks and videos in the way that nature intended.

The power button at the top-left can be programmed with an infrared signal from another remote, so you can use it to turn off your amp or TV as well. In addition, it's supremely comfortable in the hand, and we've found that the two AA batteries it needs last for months on end, too.

LOGITECH HARMONY 555

Price	£50
Internet	www.logitech.co.uk
Rating	★★★★★

Once you get more than a few remote controls on the coffee table, you can end up doing a lot of reaching and frowning – with the one sitting next to you inevitably not being the one you need. This is where universal remotes come to the rescue, and the Logitech Harmony 555 is our favourite.

Plug the Harmony into a computer using its USB connector and you'll be taken through which equipment you need to control. It will then be programmed to do just that. You can set scenarios, such as "watch DVD", and send out multiple commands, or just use it to channel browse. It's built to last and feels luxuriously weighty in the hand. You could spend a lot more cash on a flashier universal controller, but the 555 is a great place to start.

HD camcorders

What better way to use your HDTV than for your own HD movies? With HD camcorders more affordable than ever, it's a great time to buy

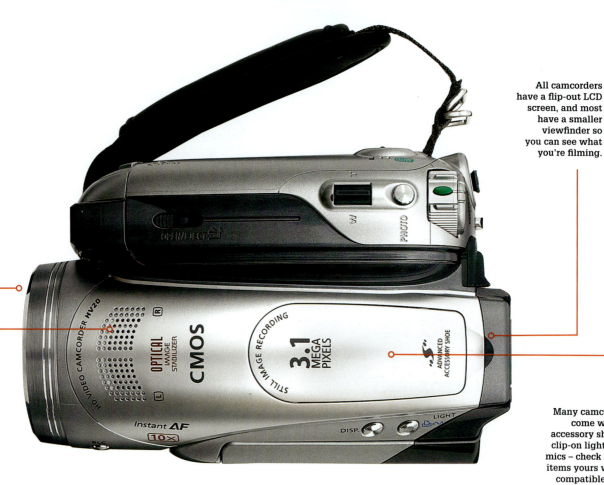

All camcorders have a flip-out LCD screen, and most have a smaller viewfinder so you can see what you're filming.

A high-quality lens can improve image quality dramatically. Some camcorders allow you to screw filters (or other lenses) onto them to create effects such as wide-angle and colour tints.

Built-in microphones tend to pick up lots of background noise, so look for a camcorder with an external microphone input.

Many camcorders come with an accessory shoe for clip-on lighting or mics – check which items yours will be compatible with.

TRIPODS

Invest in a good tripod when you buy an HD camcorder, as shaky camerawork is an instant turn-off.

Standard-definition camcorders are an easily affordable way to make your own home movies, but once you have a spanking new HDTV to watch them on, you'll notice the quality isn't all that great. Instead of sharp lines, you'll see blurred edges; instead of crisply defined textures, a blocky mess.

Fortunately, HD camcorders are no longer the preserve of those who can afford to spend £1000 plus. Now, you can buy a 720p camcorder for less than £400, as you'll see opposite. But if you want to record in 1080i, you'll need to spend more. Again, see opposite for our pick of the best.

HDV vs AVCHD

HDV camcorders use the same miniDV tapes as standard-definition camcorders, and record at a resolution of 1440 x 1080 pixels. You'll have noticed (possibly) that this isn't a widescreen aspect ratio, but the individual pixels aren't square – they have an aspect ratio of 1.33:1, which means the final image will fit perfectly onto a 16:9 HDTV.

AVCHD camcorders are a better choice for most people, since they offer a choice of 1080i or 1080p, although the latter are only just starting to appear and are costly. They record to hard disk, flash memory or DVDs, but Blu-ray models are also emerging. Eliminating tape from the equation has several advantages, not least of which is that you don't have to manually transfer the footage you've taken onto your PC in real-time. This is an irritating and time-consuming process, but with a hard disk or flash-based camcorder the MPEG-4 files can simply be copied across.

Making resolutions

It's tempting to choose a camcorder based on its resolution, but, like your HDTV itself, that would be a mistake. There are other factors that rontribute to image quality, including optics and processing, so while a higher resolution is generally a good thing, don't rely on it solely to make a buying decision.

The bit rate at which a camera records is a key consideration, too. Camcorders use compression to cram as much footage into a given space as possible, so while two models might both record MPEG-4 video at 1080i, one could produce significantly higher quality than the other if they use different bit rates. Some camcorders, for example, record at 9Mb/sec, while other MPEG-4 camcorders step that up to 19.7Mb/sec.

After shooting some footage, you can edit it for a more professional look (see p136), or simply plug your camcorder into your HDTV and press play. If you want the easy option, look for a camcorder with an HDMI output, as then it requires plugging in just a single lead.

CANON HF 10

Price:	£665
Internet:	www.canon.co.uk
Rating:	★★★★☆

The HF10 was the first camcorder to make the AVCHD format viable for the more serious videomaker. It's also the first HD camera to come with a whopping 16GB of flash memory built in – enough for two hours of footage at top quality, with an SDHC slot available too. The top recording mode of 1920 x 1080 and 17Mbits/sec data rate is about as high as you'll find, and the HF10 even includes a 25PF progressive shooting mode, for sharp framegrabs and a film-like look. Results are excellent when using preset modes (or when left in auto), but there's also a wealth of manual settings.. There are minijacks for a mic and headphones, bit no lens ring, and only Canon's proprietary 'S' Mini Advanced Shoe, which is a slight shame.

What really separates it from the pack, however, is image quality. Based around a large 1/3.2in CMOS, it captures great colour in all but the darkest conditions, and its resolution provides class-leading detail. It all adds up to a very tempting package, even at this price. If your budget doesn't quite stretch to the HF10, however, don't despair: Canon also makes an almost identical model called the HF100, which has a less fetching grey body and lacks the 16GB of flash, but it comes in at around £100 less.

SONY HDR-TG3

Price:	£493
Internet:	www.sony.co.uk
Rating:	★★★★☆

This is one of the smallest Full HD camcorders yet. It weighs under 300g, yet records at up to 1920 x 1080 using AVCHD compression. It can also shoot standard definition video, using MPEG-2. It even records 5.1 surround sound, using a trio of microphones on the top. The upright design makes it relatively comfortable to use, although the thumb-operated zoom takes a little getting used to. It's also ready to shoot very quickly. Image quality in sunny conditions has rich colours and good balance, but its small 1/5in CMOS means it's not so good in low light, with lots of grain evident.

The only real drawback is that the TG3 shoots on MemoryStick DUO Flash cards, which tend to be around twice the price of SDHC. You do get a 4GB card in the box, but that's only enough for around half an hour of footage in the top quality mode. Nevertheless, the TG3 packs a huge amount of video quality into a tiny, pocket-friendly package. It's not cheap, but it's reasonable given its talents. So if you do fancy whipping out full HD video recording from a jacket pocket, this little beauty is tailor-made for the task.

JVC GZ-MG330

Price:	£260
Internet:	www.jvc.co.uk
Rating:	★★★★★

This isn't actually an HD model, but it's certainly worth considering in the grand scheme of things, as it's a great gadget in a number of ways. Firstly, it records onto hard disk, while keeping the size and price down - it packs a healthy 30GB of storage in while remain very bag-friendly. It's also got the Laser Touch Operation system – essentially a sensitive strip down the side of the LCD to control menus, with pulsing blue lights. It's not the most precise of methods, actually, but you do at least get control over focus and exposure, as well as independent shutter control.

Since this camcorder records video at 720 x 576, and uses MPEG-2 compression at up to 8.5Mb/sec, you can fit a whopping seven hours of footage on the hard disk, or up to 37 hours if you knock image quality down a few notches. But you shouldn't, as its capable of some impressive results. Colour saturation is vibrant but natural in bright daylight and while low light footage has a yellow bias, it isn't as full of grain as you'd expect. So while this is still a budget camcorder, its seven hours of storage makes it great value for a that voyage round the world you keep meaning to get round to. You can even get it in red, silver or blue to match your outfit. And, at under 400g, it won't overburden your baggage allowance either.

TOSHIBA CAMILEO PRO HD

Price:	£180
Internet:	www.toshiba-europe.com
Rating:	★★★★★

If you thought HD camcorders came at a premium, think again: this one offers 720p shooting for under £200. Naturally, there are a few sacrifices to achieve this goal, including the 4Mb/sec compression which does introduce artefacts. And, although 128MB of memory is built in, only 90MB can be used for shooting video, which is enough for just three minutes of HD. So you'll need to factor in the price of a SDHC card, for which a slot is provided. But with that low data rate a 4GB card costing a tenner will house over two hours of footage.

Video is recorded in MP4 format, rather than AVCHD, which is far less widely supported by video editing apps, but you can burn the files to video DVD using the supplied Nero 8 Essentials, and it's also ideal for uploading to YouTube. You won't find many enthusiast features: there's no manual focusing, no manual white balance, no shutter speed setting, and little exposure control. But there is a built-in LED video light, which helps in poor illumination. Given sunnier conditions, the quality is more than acceptable at this price. So while it doesn't have the features or image quality to compete with more premium HD models. It's a great-value way to join the portable HD videomaking revolution.

HD video editing

Making your own HD movies can be easy, but here are some tips to get started - as well as the software you'll need

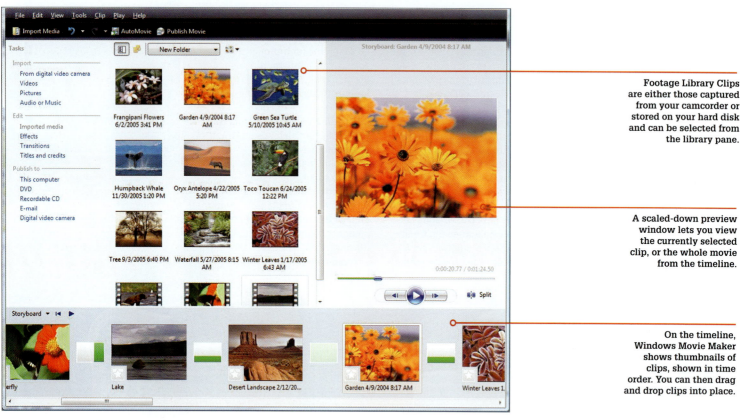

File Edit View Tools Clip Play Help

Import Media   AutoMovie   Publish Movie

Tasks

Import
  From digital video camera
  Videos
  Pictures
  Audio or Music

Edit
  Imported media
  Effects
  Transitions
  Titles and credits

Publish to
  This computer
  DVD
  Recordable CD
  E-mail
  Digital video camera

New Folder

Storyboard: Garden 4/9/2004 8:17 AM

Frangipani Flowers 6/2/2005 3:41 PM   Garden 4/9/2004 8:17 AM   Green Sea Turtle 5/10/2005 10:45 AM

Humpback Whale 11/30/2005 1:20 PM   Oryx Antelope 4/22/2005 5:20 PM   Toco Toucan 6/24/2005 12:22 PM

Tree 9/3/2005 6:40 PM   Waterfall 5/27/2005 8:15 AM   Winter Leaves 1/17/2005 6:43 AM

0:00:20.77 / 0:01:24.50

Split

Storyboard

erfly   Lake   Desert Landscape 2/12/20...   Garden 4/9/2004 8:17 AM   Winter Leaves 1.

Footage Library Clips are either those captured from your camcorder or stored on your hard disk and can be selected from the library pane.

A scaled-down preview window lets you view the currently selected clip, or the whole movie from the timeline.

On the timeline, Windows Movie Maker shows thumbnails of clips, shown in time order. You can then drag and drop clips into place.

Windows Movie Maker
The version of Movie Maker bundled with Vista Home Premium and Ultimate supports HDV.

I t's a common misconception that the more you spend on expensive, professional-quality editing software, the more your footage will resemble the latest Hollywood releases. Video-editing software is ultimately a tool, just like photo-editing applications, which can help you to improve and enhance your footage. It can't correct sloppy camerawork such as blurry, out-of-focus clips or steady wobbly, handheld shots.

All in the planning
So, before you spend hundreds of pounds on software, learn how to extract the very best quality from your camcorder. Plan what you want to see in the final video: use establishing shots for setting the scene, and even if there's no script, aim to tell a story.

Always shoot for longer than the clip will last in the final movie, as you can then trim sections later and use the extra footage for transitions. And try to avoid waving a handheld camera around in an attempt to capture everything that's going on: your audience will feel nauseous. Instead, whenever possible, mount the camera on a tripod and keep it still – the subjects will provide the action. Likewise, avoid using the zoom during a shot; set it to the appropriate level before you take the shot and leave it there. You'll be surprised how much better your shots will look.

It's in the edit
When editing, take care to choose the right settings for your project. This involves choosing the right frame rate, resolution and the correct pixel aspect ratio for your footage. Most packages have presets for HDV and AVCHD, so you just need to choose the right one. If you're going for PAL rather than full HD, the frame rate should also be 50fps.

You can sharpen video, just like photos, and also adjust the white balance and saturation in most software. Avoid placing transitions between every clip, though, as it'll make your movie look amateur – and don't overuse effects such as film grain or time-stretching for the same reasons.

Performance hog
For editing HD footage, you'll need a relatively powerful PC, and certainly one with a dual-core processor. Most HD video-editing packages recommend a 2.4GHz Intel Core 2 Duo or better, 2GB of RAM and a DirectX graphics card with at least 256MB of memory. You can make do with a lower specification, but expect sluggish performance when previewing the footage.

If you have only one camcorder and simply want to add some music and titles to your movie, there's little point in spending more than £50-£80 on editing software, and you may even be able to get away with using the Windows Movie Maker software (see above), which is built into most versions of Windows, and will do a surprising amount. If you want more control over audio and video effects, you may need to spend more. But only professionals or the well-heeled enthusiast should immediately consider forking out the hundreds of pounds that high-end applications such as Adobe Premiere Pro or Apple Final Cut will cost. 🄶

ADOBE PREMIERE ELEMENTS 7

Price	**£65**
Internet	www.adobe.co.uk
Rating	★★★★☆

A cut-down version of Adobe's professional *Premiere* package, you can choose between storyboard and timeline views. You get three tracks to play with, the Capture wizard is simple to use, and it also allows you to capture stop motion animation. The interface is easy to understand too, with tabbed windows so you can easily bring controls into view.

There are plenty of controls for enhancing your video clips, including colour correction and sharpening, plus the InstantMovie feature, which attempts to edit your footage for you, and a soundtrack generator. When the time comes to output your finished creation, you can author a DVD or Blu-ray disc, complete with menus, export Flash video and formats playable on a PlayStation Portable and iPods, as well as YouTube. It's also got some interesting online features, such as backup, and integrates brilliantly with the company's photo-editor, Photoshop Elements. Great for the beginner.

SONY VEGAS MOVIE STUDIO 9 PLATINUM

Price	**£51**
Internet	www.sonycreativesoftware.com
Rating	★★★★☆

If you're familiar with the basics of video editing already, this is an excellent choice. The main interface isn't quite as friendly as that of Pinnacle Studio – there's no storyboard view, only a timeline approach – but it's just as powerful. You can have up to four video tracks (and four audio tracks, with surround-sound) and there's a good library of effects, plus advanced three-wheel colour correction. Effects and transitions are fully customisable, allowing you to tweak their timing and other aspects exactly to your liking, and there's a decent autoscore facility too.

For beginners, there are Show Me How animated guides that teach you how to use the core functions, getting you up and running. You can also save money by downloading it directly, and you should also consider upgrading to the 'Platinum Pro Pack', which adds in more audio editing features and sound effects for another £15.

COREL VIDEOSTUDIO PRO X2

Price	**£59**
Internet	www.corel.co.uk
Rating	★★★★☆

The follow-up to Ulead's Video Studio 11, this retains its fantastic ease of use and surprising level of power. This version adds increased flexibility, with resizable windows and much stronger compatibility with the AVCHD format, plus support for BDMV files from Blu-ray camcorders.

The workflow is a three-stage Capture / Edit / Share process: at its simplest, clips can be set on a single 'film strip' and joined together with transitions. But you can also flip into timeline mode and use a second track for more complex transitions or titles, with a separate tracks for audio.

A wide range of effects are available to jazz up your compositions, including an interesting annotation tool, and a huge number of output options to get them onto DVD, Blu-ray or a generous selection of mobile devices – as well as an option for YouTube. There's also a Movie Wizard for putting together rough cuts to a basic template and a handy DV tape to DVD convertor for archival. It all adds up to a quick and easy option, although the more experimental and ambitious editor may find the lack of control over video effects a little restricting.

PINNACLE STUDIO 12 ULTIMATE

Price	**£61**
Internet	www.pinnaclesys.com
Rating	★★★★★

Using the tried-and-tested Capture, Edit, Make Movie layout, this software makes the process as simple as it can be. As with Premiere Elements and VideoStudio, you can resize the different windows to suit.

It supports HDV and AVCHD, but you can also import SD footage and upscale it afterwards. There are sophisticated tools for cleaning up audio and video, plus colour correction and lots of controls for speeding video up or down, and chroma keying – there's even a green sheet to use as a background, which you can then change to a still image or other video.

There's a new Montage feature, providing welcome effects to spruce up your creations, and a SmartMovie function that can order your clips, insert transitions and music, giving a finished production in minutes. The Scorefitter application generates music on-the-fly to the length of your movie and alters the intensity of it to match the action. Aside from the weak titling element, it's a strong contender for the first-time editor. Pinnacle Studio 12 is available in several versions, but for enthusiasts Ultimate is well worth the extra premium.

Glossary

1080i /1080p
➥ A screen or video signal with a resolution of 1920 x 1080 pixels. The 'p' stands for progressive scan, meaning each video frame is transmitted whole, whereas the 'i' refers to the interlaced version.

16:9
➥ See Aspect ratio.

4:3
➥ See Aspect ratio.

5.1, 7.1-channel
➥ Notation for speaker systems, with the first number referring to the number of satellite speakers, and the second to the presence of a dedicated bass subwoofer. Stereo audio can be referred to as two-channel, 2.0 or 2.1.

720p
➥ A screen or video signal with a resolution of 1280 x 720 pixels. The 'p' stands for progressive scan, meaning each video frame is transmitted whole.

802.11a/b/g/n
➥ The official name for Wi-Fi or WLAN. 802.11a is an older, business-related standard, with 802.11b/g being the most common standard on more recent equipment. 802.11n is the latest (and most expensive) version, with its much faster speed making it the best choice for HD streaming over home networks.

Anamorphic video
➥ A technique for compressing a 16:9 widescreen image onto a 4:3 format medium. A non-anamorphic widescreen disc will be letterboxed on a 4:3 TV, and has black borders all around it when seen on a 16:9 TV. Anamorphic transfers, however, will display at the correct aspect ratio on both 4:3 and 16:9 displays. The disadvantage is that, when on a 4:3 TV, it will often show artefacts unless the TV has a vertical compression feature.

ANSI lumens
➥ Light-output specification used to measure the brightness of projection systems more exactly than undefined lumens. 600 to 7000 or more ANSI lumens is the normal range for both DLP or LCD projectors.

Artefacts
➥ Unwanted objects in video caused by problems with signal reception, or by the picture-processing system in your TV.

Aspect ratio
➥ The ratio of width to height on an image or screen. Traditional 'square' TVs used a 4:3 (1.33:1) ratio, but modern TVs (and most broadcasts) are in the wider 16:9 ratio (1.78:1). The latter is much better suited to displaying anamorphic video, and is closer to that of cinefilm, which is even wider (up to 2.66:1) .

AV
➥ Audiovisual. An over-arching term describing any kind of equipment or technology that involves sound or moving images.

Bit rate
➥ A measurement of speed for data, either during transmission or processing. Digital video formats typically have bit rates that are measured in megabits per second (see also Mb/sec). The bit rate for DVD playback is around 10Mb/sec, whereas for HDTV broadcasts it's 19.4Mb/sec or more.

Black level
➥ A description of how well a display copes with black – on an LCD panel, this is essentially how well it can shut off the backlight to produce crisper shadows and greater detail.

Brightness
➥ Confusingly, this actually refers to black levels – this is what you'll be adjusting on a TV's brightness control (see also contrast)

Burn-in
⮑ A problem with CRT and plasma displays, when a static image is burnt into the phosphor coating, leaving faint impressions onscreen. Less common on newer sets.

Blu-ray
⮑ Sony's high-definition candidate to replace DVD, using blue rather than red lasers. Single-layer discs store 25GB, and dual-layer 50GB. The winner of the format war with HD DVD, although its use has yet to become widespead.

Chrominance
⮑ Information carried in a video signal about colour.

Coaxial
⮑ A type of cable, typically used to carry cable or terrestrial TV signals. A copper core is surrounded by an insulating material, plus a thicker conducting wire – often in the form of copper braiding – encased in a protective sheath.

Codecs
⮑ A computer algorithm used to encode/decode data, removing unnecessary information and reducing file size.

Colour temperature
⮑ A measurement, expressed in degrees Kelvin, of grey levels between black to white, with 'warmer' shades containing more yellow, and 'cooler' more blue. 6500K is typically the best setting in the home, but TVs often ship at 7000K to12000K to make them look brighter in showrooms. Most have a selectable colour temperature setting, using either figures or terms such as warm, standard and cool.

Colour wheel
⮑ A spinning wheel that sits in front of the lamp in single-chip DLP front- and rear-projection systems (see p28). Each section contains a gel to filter the light into red, green, and blue components, which are then combined to create the picture. The speed at which the wheel spins is a major factor in how prevalent the dreaded 'rainbow effect' is.

Component video
⮑ Splits the video signal into three parts (one brightness and two colour signals) over three cables, terminating

at each end in an RCA jack. In comparison to composite video, component can carry more accurate colour information and invariably produces a better picture. It's a better option than S-Video, too, and the preferred analogue choice when available. Most HD-capable TVs will only accept video signals of up to 1080i over component video, though.

Composite video
⮑ Combines luminance (brightness) and chrominance (colour) information into a single signal, carried over a single cable, terminating at each end in a RCA jack. Better than a raw RF signal, but a poor choice compared to S-Video or, even better, component video or digital formats like HDMI.

Contrast
⮑ White level (see also brightness)

Contrast ratio
⮑ This is the difference between the brightest whites and the darkest blacks a TV is capable of displaying, expressed as XXX:1. The higher the first number, the greater the ability of the display should be to show subtlety of colour, as well as overcome any ambient light in the room. It's an important factor to consider in all types of TV and projection.

CRT (cathode-ray tube)
⮑ The traditional 'picture tube' TV. This contains a vacuum tube with an electron gun at the back beam, which scans down the back side of a phosphor-coated screen, lighting up lines of phosphor dots inside the glass tube. With hundreds of these lines being updated every fraction of a second, moving images can be displayed.

Compression
⮑ Used generically to describe any technology that compresses data in a smaller space. There are two principle types: lossy and lossless. Lossless compression is used when all the original material must be retained in its original form, whereas lossy compression can be employed in digital images, audio or video. By using methods of deciding which data may be discarded, it keeps down file sizes at the risk of increasing errors. Examples of lossy compression include MP3 audio and MPEG video files.

Deinterlacing
⮑ The process of converting an interlaced video signal to a progressive-scan signal; combining separate, interlaced fields into a single full frame. This is often done by the TV itself, or by progressive-scan equipment, such as DVD or Blu-ray players.

DivX
⮑ A compressed video format common to video distributed online, and with a strong future in digital download services. Based on the MPEG4 standard, it's sufficiently effective to allow a feature-length movie to fit on a CD, albeit with potentially distracting compression artefacts.

DLP (digital light processing)
⮑ A projection technique using thousands of tiny mirrors (one for each pixel), which swivel to control the amount of light they reflect. Two basic types exist: single-chip, which uses a spinning colour wheel to separate the primary colours, and pricier three-chip projectors, with a separate chip for red, green and blue. DLP avoids the 'screen door' effect of LCD projectors and is capable of better black levels.

Dolby Digital
➲ A multichannel digital audio format. Commonly, this is in a 5.1 configuration, although a 'Dolby Digital' soundtrack can actually be anything from 1 to 5.1 channels. Also known as AC-3. Also comes in Digital Plus and TrueHD variants (*see p114*).

Downscaling
➲ The process of scaling down a higher resolution input to a lower resolution, such as a 1080i input being displayed on a standard-definition TV. Also known as downconversion.

DTS
➲ A digital surround-sound format used in both domestic and cinema environments. Not as common as Dolby Digital, but commonly considered to produce a higher-quality output. Also comes in DTS-HD high-resolution audio and DTS-HD Master Audio variants (*see p114*).

DVI (digital visual interface)
➲ A computer-style connection used to carry video signals from high-resolution source components to compatible TVs or computer monitors. Most – but not all – DVI connections support HDCP (High-bandwidth Digital Content Protection), although DVI connectors are increasingly being replaced by HDMI, which is capable of carrying both video and audio.

DRM (digital rights management)
➲ A generic term for technologies that allow copyright owners to specify what can be done with a piece of intellectual property, such as a music or video file. Often, this will be used to tie a downloaded file to a particular computer, or to prevent files from being duplicated (*see p83*).

DVB-T, DVB-S
➲ The Digital Video Broadcasting system used to receive digital television in Europe. The T-variant is that used by Freeview tuners (T= Terrestrial), and the S-variant the lesser-used Satellite version.

Energy Star compliance
➲ An energy efficiency certification for consumer electronics. Compliant products need to meet stringent standards for power consumption in standby mode.

EPG (electronic programme guide)
➲ A listing of available TV channels with current and future programmes, from a set-top box or PVR. Generally presented as an onscreen grid and often allowing scheduled recordings to be made.

Ethernet
➲ A networking protocol, whose sockets are commonly found on computer equipment and increasingly on AV products, such as network-capable Blu-ray and HD DVD players. It comes in two forms – fast Ethernet (10/100) and gigabit Ethernet (10/100/1000) – with the latter offering much faster transfer speeds.

FireWire
➲ An external bus standard, originally developed by Apple and often found on computers and camcorders. There are several generations, including FireWire 400, FireWire 800, with the nomenclature denoting the speed – for example, 400Mb/sec. Also called IEEE 1394 or i-Link.

Flat-panel TV
➲ Another name for plasma or LCD TVs.

Frame rate
➲ The speed at which frames are displayed – for example, 24 complete frames per second (24fps) in the case of film, and 50 interlaced frames per second in the case of PAL.

Frame
➲ A complete picture in a video signal, containing all of the picture's scanning lines. An interlaced frame contains only half of these lines, whereas a progressive scan frame contains the entirety.

Freeview
➲ The marketing name for the free digital TV channels broadcast over the DVB-T system in the UK.

Full HD
➲ Another term for a 1080p screen or video signal.

Ghosting
➲ A common problem with older LCD sets where an image moves faster than the display can redraw it. This leaves a trail of former versions in the wake of the redrawn image, causing it to appear blurred.

HDCP (High-Bandwidth Digital Content Protection)
➲ Used in high-resolution signals over digital DVI and HDMI connection recordings, aimed at preventing unauthorised duplication of copyright material. Without a complete path being HDCP protected, the device will res or refuse to play across a digital output.

HD DVD
➲ Principally developed by Toshiba, it was an HD candidate to replace DVD, using blue rather than red lasers. It was formally discontinued in March 2008 after the majority of industry support aligned behind Blu-ray.

HDMI (high-definition multimedia interface)
■ A multipin interface designed to transfer uncompressed digital video (with HDCP) and multichannel audio along

a single cable. HDMI is also backward-compatible with most DVI connections through the use of an adapter.

HDTV (high-definition television)
⮑ Although it's often used as a generic description of all digital televisions, HDTV more accurately refers to the highest set of resolutions. There's no universal agreement on this, but it's generally assumed to mean either 720p (progressive scan) format or 1080-line interlaced or progressive scan variants (1080i or 1080p). There's some debate over whether 720i (interlaced) can be considered a true HD format.

HDTV ready
⮑ A term used to describe a TV capable of showing at least a 720p video signal without downscaling.

Horizontal resolution
⮑ The number of pixels that can be resolved across the width of an image. Whereas the horizontal resolution of analogue sources was as low as 240 pixels for VCRs and 540 pixels for DVD players, HD formats use 1280 or 1920 lines for 720p and 1080i/p respectively.

IEEE 1394
⮑ See FireWire.

Interlaced scan signal
⮑ In an interlaced scan, the picture is reassembled from a series of video signals, with the odd lines displayed first, then the even lines following so rapidly that the eye sees just a single, composited image. This approach requires substantially less bandwidth than progressive scan, as images are only redrawn every other frame, and only half the information is displayed at any one time – but it can result in motion blur or smearing.

Keystone correction
⮑ A method of correcting unevenness when a projector isn't facing directly on to the screen. While severe distortions can generally be overcome, this is liable to introduce a softening of detail at extreme settings.

LCD (Liquid Crystal Display)
⮑ One of the methods used to create flat-panel TVs. A set of fluorescent bulbs is placed behind a liquid crystal matrix. This consists of two polarising transparent panels with a liquid crystal solution sandwiched in between. With a red, green and blue element for each pixel, these are controlled individually to either let light through or not, with the pattern of transparent and dark crystals forming the image. Also used in some projectors.

Letterboxed video
⮑ Black bars at the top and bottom of an image when, for example, watching a cinefilm print transferred to 16:9

widescreen, widescreen video on a 4:3 aspect TV, or non-anamorphic widescreen on a widescreen TV.

Lumens
⮑ See ANSI lumens.

Luminance
⮑ Information carried in a video signal about brightness.

Mb/sec (megabits per second)
⮑ Not to be confused with MB/sec, this is generally used in networking bandwidth or data transmission. It's expressed in millions of binary bits per second.

MB/sec (megabytes per second)
⮑ Often used when expressing the speed of file or data transfers. A megabyte is 1,048,576 bytes, making 1MB/sec equivalent to 8Mb/sec.

MHz (megahertz)
⮑ One million cycles per second. Often used when expressing bandwidth in video signals, or the speed of computer processors.

MPEG
⮑ An acronym of the Moving Picture Experts Group, MPEG is also used to represent a set of media-compression standards. MPEG-1 is a largely legacy format, and is most commonly found in CD-ROMs. MPEG-2 is prevalent used in video formats, including DVD and Blu-ray, while the newer MPEG-4 is often used online for low-bandwidth applications (*see p96*).

Native resolution
➲ Flat-panel displays have a fixed resolution, denoting the number of pixels that make them up and expressed as the number of horizontal pixels by the number of vertical pixels. Video signals with resolutions other than this must be upscaled or downscaled to the screen correctly. This will happen in the case of a 720p signal being shown on a 1080p TV or vice versa.

NTSC
➲ The American equivalent of PAL, this analogue standard is being replaced by digital ATSC, just as PAL is being replaced by DVB in the UK.

PAL
➲ The analogue broadcast television standard for the UK and many other European countries. PAL broadcasts use 625 horizontal lines of resolution per frame, and display at 50 interlaced frames per second. The PAL system is gradually being replaced by the newer digital DVB standard.

Pan-and-scan
➲ When a widescreen movie is transferred to a 4:3 aspect ratio, extra cuts, pans or zooms are added in order to keep action or text clearly displayed. While this results in a full-screen showing, it also leads to a significant amount of lost picture information, principally at either end of the picture.

PIP (picture-in-picture)
➲ Where two input signals are overlaid onto each other, so they're both viewable on the same screen. True picture-in-picture consists of a small inset image overlaid on the main image, although the move to widescreen aspect ratios has also bought in 'split screen' designs that are also referred to as POP (picture-outside-picture) or PAP (picture-and-picture).

Pixel
➲ A single point on a LCD or plasma screen, or on a CRT monitor, each consisting of a set of red, green and blue dots. The smaller the size of each pixel, the more detail can be resolved, and the more pixels making up an image the greater the resolution. A contraction of 'picture element'.

Pixel response time
➲ This refers to the amount of time (in milliseconds or ms) it takes for a single pixel in a LCD panel to switch from black to white to black again. Be careful, though, as some manufacturers quote the grey-to-grey response time.

Plasma
➲ One of the principle technologies used in flat-panel televisions. Two transparent glass panels have a thin layer of pixels sandwiched in between, effectively as millions of tiny fluorescent bulbs. Each pixel is composed of three gas-filled cells (sub-pixels of red, green and blue). An electric current can be applied to each of these, causing the gas inside them to ionise and emit UV light, stimulating the cells' phosphors and creating a lit image.

Progressive scan
➲ Unlike interlaced video, which splits frames into two fields to keep bandwidth down, progressive-scan video displays the entire frame in a single pass. This results in a smoother picture and finer detail, but requires more bandwidth, as it needs to contain twice as much vertical information.

PVR (personal video recorder)
➲ A device or software program that can record television via the use of an EPG and either a hard disk or DVD recorder. These often include features such as being able to schedule the recording of an entire series with a single button, or pausing live television broadcasts (*see p102*). Also known as DVRs (digital video recorders).

QoS (Quality of Service)
➲ A feature on wireless networks that prioritises sensitive traffic (such as streaming HD video), so that more sporadic data (such as web surfing) doesn't interrupt the flow of video information (*see p120*).

Rainbow effect
➲ A side-effect of DLP projection systems, where the rapid succession of red, green and blue images can become visible as a rainbow-like flash when the viewer moves their eyes across the screen. Strangely, not everyone is affected by this, and even then it often only proves to be a minor distraction. Newer systems use techniques such as spinning the colour wheel much faster in order to minimise the effect.

RCA
➲ Originally designed to carry audio from phonograph players to amplifiers during the 1950s, RCA sockets and cables have since been adopted for use in a wide range of applications. This includes component and composite video connections and the transfer of digital audio. Also known as phono connectors.

Rear-projection TV
➲ Common in the US, these TVs use a projector situated behind (or underneath) an opaque screen to create an image larger than traditional CRT displays could manage. Complex reflection and cooling systems often resulted in cabinets of a significant size, though, thus limiting their appeal in smaller European living rooms.

Resolution
➲ Described in analogue terms as 'lines' or, in the context of digital displays, pixels, the true visible resolution of an

image depends on both your display and the resolution of the source video signal.

Response time
⮞ See pixel response time.

RF (radio frequency) jack
⮞ Also known as a '75ohm coaxial' connection, this jack can carry video and stereo audio simultaneously. Often used for bringing raw signals from aerials to tuners, such as those in a set-top box, VCR or TV, it's inferior to composite, S-Video and component video when it comes to connecting components and should be avoided.

Saturation
⮞ The amount of colour present in an image, with zero saturation equating to black-and-white, and over-saturation leading to garish or overblown colouration.

Scart
⮞ A 21-pin connector, commonly found on VCRs and DVD players, as well as practically any TV you'll buy. It can optionally carry S-Video or RGB video signals (as well as audio), although not all signal types are always supported.

Screen-door effect
⮞ When the fine lines that separate a projector's pixels become visible in the projected image.

SDTV (standard-definition television)
⮞ Another way of describing TV formats lower than 720i, such as PAL or DVB.

Set-top box
⮞ A standalone box containing a tuner for analogue cable, digital cable, DVB-T or satellite broadcasts. TVs with just an analogue tuner will need a set-top box to receive either free-to-air terrestrial (Freeview) or satellite (Freesat) once the analogue broadcast system is switched off (see p16).

Subwoofer
⮞ A dedicated bass speaker, typically used to transmit sounds below 40Hz in movie soundtracks.

S-Video
⮞ A four-pin connector that carries the chrominance and luminance portions of a video signal separately in order to reduce interference. Direct S-Video connections generally outperform composite, but are inferior to component or digital connections.

TFT
⮞ An acronym for Thin Film Transistor, these are the individual switches used to control each pixel in a LCD. Also used as a generic term for LCD televisions and computer monitors (see p24).

Throw ratio
⮞ Referring to projectors, this is the ratio between the projection distance and the width of the image. For

example, a throw ratio of 1.8:1 means that the projector must be 1.8m away from the screen to result in an image measuring 1m across.

Tube TV
⮞ See CRT.

UPnP (Universal Plug 'n' Play)
⮞ A networking standard that means digital devices are able to talk to each other on a common basis. UPnP also comes in a more complex AV variant that guarantees a level of interoperability with media playback and streaming equipment.

Upscaling
⮞ The term for scaling a lower resolution video signal to a higher one. This can increase either the number of pixels, frame rate and/or deinterlacing, by interpolating existing pixels or frames and adding new ones to create the new format. Also referred to as upconverting or line-doubling (see p70).

VCR
⮞ Video cassette recorder.

Vertical resolution
⮞ The number of horizontal pixels that can be resolved across the height of an image. On analogue (PAL) sources, horizontal resolution varies by source, but the vertical resolution is always 625 lines – some of which is used to carry extra information, such as Teletext pages and subtitles. Digital signals have vertical resolutions ranging from 720 lines for 720p to 1080 lines for 1080p.

Viewing angle
⮞ Usually expressed in degrees, this is an approximation of the angle at which the TV picture diminishes significantly in brightness or contrast. 180 degrees is the theoretical maximum, although few sets manage even close to this. Generally, it's the more important horizontal (side-to-side) viewing angle that's used, but vertical viewing angles are also important in some circumstances.

Widescreen
⮞ See aspect ratio.

Wi-Fi/wireless/WLAN
⮞ A generic term for wireless networking technology – mainly the 802.11 networking protocols used by computers and networked media players. ⓖ

Useful phone numbers

For more information, or some brochures to leaf through, why not pick up the ol' dog and bone?

A

AAD 01327 706560
Absolute Analogue 020 8459 8113
Absolute Sounds 020 8971 3909
Acoustic Energy 01285 654432
Acoustic Research 023 9269 0999
Adobe 020 7365 0733
Aiwa 0870 168 9000
Akai 020 7887 7780
Alba 0870 873 0079
Altec Lansing 0870 458 0011
Apple 0800 048 0408
ARC Acoustics 01638 721237
Arcam 01223 203203
Atacama 01455 283251
ATC 01285 760561
Atlas 01563 524320
ATMT 0870 410 2868
Audica 01480 839 239
Audio Illusion 01753 542761
Audio Synergy 01924 406016
Audiophile Furniture 01892 619319
Audio Technica 0113 277 1441
Audusa 020 8241 9826
AVI 01453 752656
Avid 01480 457300
AVM 01252 510363

B

B&W 01903 221 500
BADA (British Audio Dealers Association) 0800 915 8589
Bang & Olufsen 01189 692288
Base 01892 619319
BBG Distribution 0845 600 4224
Belkin 0845 607 7787
BenQ 01442 301000
Beyerdynamic 01444 258258
Black Rhodium 01332 342233
Bose 08707 414500
Boston 01285 650814

Bryston 08704 441044
BT 0800 917 7611
Buffalo 0845 351 1005
Bush 0870 873 0079

C

Cadence 020 7738 4911
Cambridge Audio 0845 900 1230
Canon 01737 220000
Canton 023 9250 1888
Castle 01756 795333
Celestion 01622 687442
Cerwin Vega 01582 690600
Chord Company 01980 625700
Chord Electronics 01622 721444
Clearaudio 01252 702705
Clearer Audio 01702 543981
Crane Audio 08704 441056
Creative Labs 0118 982 8200
Creek 01442 260146
CSE 01423 359054
Cyberhome 02392 697305
Cyberlink 0870 027 0985
Cymbol 01256 381569
Cyrus 01480 435 577

D

Daewoo 0870 100 2525
Dali 0845 644357
Deadrock 01444 248873
Denon 01234 741 200
Densen +45 7518 1214
Devolo 01865 244141
DigiFusion 0870 606 0044
D-link 020 8955 9000
Dolby Labs 01793 842100
Domia 01844 337803
Dynaudio 020 7378 1810
Dynavector 01665 830862

E

Earmax 020 8882 2822
Ecosse 01563 558893
Eltax 01327 860789
Epson 08702 416900
EsotericAudio 01480 453791
Evesham 0870 160 9500

F

Fujitsu 020 8731 3450
Fujitsu Siemens 0845 678 0172

G

Gale 0870 900 1000
Gecko 020 8603 0480
Gigabyte 01908 362700
Goodmans 0870 873 0080

H

Hannspree 0871 666 0850
Harbeth 01444 484371
Harman-Kardon 020 8731 4670
Heco 023 9269 0999
Helios 01579 363603
Heybrook 01752 848816
Hi-fi Direct 020 7827 9827
HP 0845 270 4222
Hitachi 01628 643000
Humax 020 8547 4240

I

IAG 0845 458 0011
Infocus 0800 028 6470
Intempo 0161 828 5218
Isotek 01635 291357
Ixos 01844 219012

J

Jamo 0845 600 4224
JBL 020 8731 4670
Joytech 0800 3899 647
JPW 01752 848816
JVC 020 8450 3282

K

KEF 01622 672261
Kenwood 01923 816444
Klegg 0870 075 5344
Koch Media 0870 027 0985
Koss 01256 374700

L

Lecson 020 7408 4444
Lektropacks 08700 711911
LFD 01255 422533
LG 01753 500400
Limit 08452 261619
Linksys 0800 026 1418
Lindy 01642 754000
Linn 0500 888909
Loewe 0800 027 6465
Logic3 020 8902 4422
Logitech 01753 870900
London Decca 01444 461611
Loricraft 01488 72267
Lowthe 020 8300 9166
Lynwood Electronics 01709 875408

INTRO | CHOOSING | BUYING | SETTING UP | ENJOYING HD | HD ON YOUR PC | EXPANSION | HD HOME

HDTV
and home entertainment

Editor
Ross Burridge
editor@igizmo.co.uk

Brand Art Editor
Russell Clark

Production
Martin James
Priti Patel

Photography
Jaimie McGovern

Artwork
Linda Duong, Mike Harding,
Magic Torch, Mike Mansfield

Contributors
Seth Barton, David Bayon, Jon Bray, James Billington,
Barry Collins, Fahim Chowdury, Tim Danton,
Jon Goody, Will Head, Kenneth Hemphill, Dave Ludlow
Jim Martin, Dave Stevenson

Ad Production Controller
Michael Hills 020 7907 6129

Print
Printed by BGP, Bicester, Oxfordshire

International Licensing
Content is available for licensing overseas.
Contact Winnie Liesenfeld
00 44 20 7907 6134
winnie_liesenfeld@dennis.co.uk

Publishing Director
Bruce Sandell

Group Advertising Director
Julie Price
020 7907 6660 julie_price@dennis.co.uk

Bookazine Manager
Dharmesh Mistry
dharmesh_mistry@dennis.co.uk

Circulation Director
Martin Belson

Finance Director
Brett Reynolds

Group Finance Director
Ian Leggett

Chief Executive
James Tye

Chairman
Felix Dennis

Turned on to technology

iGIZMO

Sign up for the magazine...
www.igizmo.co.uk